The Possibilities Organization— The New Science of Possibilities Management

Robert R. Carkhuff, Ph.D.
and
Bernard G. Berenson, Ph.D.

Contributors:
Don Benoit, M.A.
Christopher Carkhuff, M.A. Cert.

Published by Possibilities Publishing
22 Amherst Road
Amherst, MA 01002
413-253-3488
1-800-822-2801
413-253-3490 (fax)
www.possibilitiespublisher.com

ISBN 0-87425-577-5

Editorial services by Mary George
Production services by Jean Miller
Cover design by Donna Thibault-Wong

This book is dedicated to John T. Kelly, Manager, IBM's Office of the Future, who conducted the first private-sector research on the interdependent organizational relationships of Human, Information, and Organizational Capital Development.

The Possibilities Organization—
The New Science of Possibilities Management

CONTENTS

About the Authors

DR. ROBERT R. CARKHUFF is Founder and Chairperson, The Carkhuff Group: Human Technology, Inc., Human Resource Development Press, Inc., and Carkhuff Thinking Systems, Inc. One of the most frequently referenced writers in the social sciences, Dr. Carkhuff has authored many major works, including *The Age of the New Capitalism,* and *The Possibilities Schools.*

DR. BERNARD G. BERENSON is Executive Director, Carkhuff Institute of Applied Science and Human Technology. A professor at the state universities of Maryland, Massachusetts, and New York, Dr. Berenson was co-founder of the original Center for Human Resource Development and chairperson of its graduate training program at American International College. He is the author of *The Possibilities Mind* and many other books.

Together, Carkhuff and Berenson have introduced several market revolutions over the past four decades. They brought us the first interpersonal skills system in the '60s and '70s. They introduced the first individual models of human resource development in the '70s and '80s. Their combined efforts also initiated us into twenty-first-century thinking *in the '80s* with the first models of new leadership and organizational capital development. Now, as creators of *The New Science of Possibilities,* Carkhuff and Berenson are the first scientists to address the area of management. *The Possibilities Organization* is their contribution to all possibilities managers and leaders.

About the Contributors

DON BENOIT is Director, Educational Projects, Carkhuff Thinking Systems, Inc., and contributor to Chapter 5, Managing Information Capital Development, and Chapter 6, Managing Mechanical Capital Development.

CHRISTOPHER CARKHUFF is Director, Research and Development, Carkhuff Thinking Systems, Inc., and contributor to Chapter 3, Managing Organizational Capital Development.

Foreword

by Barry Cohen, Ph.D.
Vice President, Marketing
Parametric Technology Corporation

In **The Possibilities Leader,** Carkhuff and Berenson introduced us to the universal language of processing. They taught us how to process interdependently so that we can generate new and powerful images of phenomena and innovate within phenomena. They labeled their interdependent processing system "I^5" to represent the different human and information processing systems involved, and showed how "I^5" systems empower us to generate new images of any phenomena—people, data, or things. The authors also demonstrated how we can live inside of these phenomena and generate totally new phenomenal operations.

Now, in **The Possibilities Organization**, Carkhuff and Berenson demonstrate how they live, learn, and work within, between, and among organizations. They "I^5" with organizations, becoming *"one"* with them in order to generate new and powerful images of organizational possibilities. In so doing, they deliver to us the first systematic approach to birthing and growing organizations with infinite possibilities. Organizations will never be the same!

The Possibilities Organization is a book about a *"paradigm shift"* in management from probabilities science to possibilities science—although, in truth, current management practices hardly qualify as a paradigm, let alone a science! *Scientific management,* the platform upon which twentieth-century probabilities management was based, is no more than a euphemism for totalitarian rule: command and control policy, classist organizations, conditioned personnel, and the rest. *Possibilities management*, then, is more than a paradigm shift: it is the first authentic management paradigm, the first model that actually defines all of the processing systems required by the twenty-first-century manager, and all of the new capital development functions to which those systems are dedicated.

First, let us take a brief look at the processing systems:

I^1 Information relating systems to define phenomenal operations;

I^2 Information representing systems to dimensionalize images of phenomena;

I^3 Individual processing systems to generate new images of phenomena;

I^4 Interpersonal processing systems to generate more powerful images of phenomena;

I^5 Interdependent processing systems to generate the most powerful images of phenomena.

Interdependently and synergistically related, these processing systems define the core of the manager's contribution to any phenomena, especially *tasks-in-mind*.

Next, let us view the organizational functions to which the processing is dedicated. They are labeled "new capital development systems" to represent their contributions in the equation for generating wealth. There are five functions in all:

MCD   Marketplace capital development, or continuous marketplace positioning;

OCD   Organizational capital development, or continuous organizational alignment;

HCD   Human capital development, or continuous human processing;

ICD   Information capital development, or continuous information modeling;

mCD   Mechanical capital development, or continuous mechanical tooling.

When the interdependent processing systems are dedicated to organizational functions, they generate new capital development. For the first time in the history of business, managers know what they are doing and where they are going. We have a real paradigm to guide us!

But this book does more than simply present a paradigm. It builds a bridge that spans not only probabilities and possibilities science, but also probabilities and possibilities *culture*. The authors empower us to actualize a culture of true freedom: genuine free-enterprise-driven economies, truly free and direct democratic governance, all empowered by free scientific processing systems—by, in a word, *"process-centricity."*

In a *process-centric* culture, everything is processing. There is no enduring content. One processor's outputs are another's inputs. All processors' interdependent processing is spiraling and changing, as are the phenomena that they process. In short, processing is an accelerator of evolution wherein we can continuously influence our continuously changing destinies.

In a process-centric culture, all models of processing are powerful and elegant. As the authors demonstrate, even the formula for generating wealth can be reduced to simple yet potent terms:

$$\mathbf{I}^5 \longleftrightarrow \mathbf{NCD}$$

I^5 represents the interdependent processing systems of possibilities management. NCD represents the organization's new capital development systems, which generate wealth. I^5 and NCD are related interdependently and synergistically: each contributes to the other's growth. We managers may now become *process-centric* in a wealth-generating culture!

*Possibilities leaders
generate
possibilities organizations.*

Preface
The Requirements of the
Twenty-First Century

At least twice in the last decade, the clarion cries of false prophets have been trumpeted. Ten years ago, the Soviet Union was still planning to bury Western capitalism. Indeed, the Soviets pitted their planning systems against our processing systems. The rest is history.

Up until a few years ago, the Japanese were claiming that the twenty-first century would be the Asian century, led by them, of course. We know this personally because they adopted our platform on *"The New Capitalism,"* believing that they had the superior brainpower needed to dominate the new century. To be sure, they posed their imitative systems against our generative and innovative systems. And lost!

Now many in the unfree world are saying that the free market has failed. Wrong! The unfree nations have failed. They have failed because their cultures have failed. Their cultures have failed because they have been bound by past traditions—dysfunctional traditions. They cannot participate in a free, global market with command and control economies. They cannot generate free-enterprise-driven economies with authoritarian governance. They cannot implement free democratic governance without new sources of generating wealth—what we label *"new capital development."*

Sometime in the last decade of the twentieth century, civilization crossed a momentous threshold. It moved from shaping cultures based upon past traditions to generating cultures to meet future requirements. Because of spiraling changes in technology-driven economies, the historic traditions no longer suffice. Scientific and technological *"breakthroughs"* have generated robust, new socioeconomic requirements that must be met in order to participate in the marketplace. Our traditional responses, no matter how enduring, are rendered impotent. The requirements that define our new century's culture are prepotent.

The standards for the global economy in the twenty-first century are already defined. They were defined by the Western economies in the last decade as:

> 1. Free-Market Economies,
> 2. Free Democratic Governance,
> 3. New Capital Development Systems.

Let us state this in the form of a principle:

Free-market economies are accomplished by free democratic governance empowered by new capital development systems.

It is the Western mission to define these growthful socioeconomic standards for the global economy in the twenty-first century. Let us elaborate.

By "free-market economies," we do not simply mean capitalism as it has been practiced historically. Here in the United States, for example, we continue to practice a mixed form of capitalism and socialism. We seek deregulation when that pleases us and government subsidies when that supports us. By "free market," we mean entrepreneurial- and intrapreneurial-driven capitalistic economies. We mean economies driven by the generative and innovative processing of free people. We mean risk-taking entrepreneurs rather than note-taking bureaucrats.

There must be some good reason for the sources of spiraling change in the last decade. Ninety percent of the *breakthroughs* in science and technology have occurred in the last decade. Yes, 90 percent of the *breakthroughs* in the history of humankind! And 90 percent of these *breakthroughs* have been generated by Western science and enterprise!

These free-market economic systems are enabled by the truly free and enlightened citizenry of free democratic governance. By "free democratic governance," we do not simply mean democracy as it has been practiced historically. In the United States, for example, we continue to practice representative democracy—meaning that every politician is in business for himself or herself. Politicians do not represent their constituencies; they represent the monies that support them. However, we now have the electronic means to become a direct democracy: everyone can be educated to vote directly on every issue. It is thus time to stop the circus in Washington as well as within our corporations. By "free democratic governance," we mean true democracy within both the professional political arena and the corporation.

The free-market economic systems, then, are accomplished by free democratic governance. This entire freeing system is enabled by new capital development systems. By "new capital development," we mean new wealth-generating sources. "Capital" merely means what is *most important.* There are new capital sources of wealth. To be sure, financial capital plays an important, catalytic role in generating wealth. It accounts for about 10 percent to 15 percent of the variability in economic productivity growth. It is necessary but not sufficient for wealth generation. What we would like to present in this book are other sources of wealth, the new capital development systems.

The first of these new capital development systems is **marketplace capital development.** Marketplace capital is the impact of the positioning of our corporation in the marketplace. In other words, we position our corporations for differentiation in the marketplace. This positioning is the source of our comparative advantage or competitive edge. Now let us ask:

> How many of you believe that your corporations'
> marketplace positioning is the most critical
> source of corporate success?

We have challenged many executives on this issue of marketplace positioning. To a person, they have agreed that 99 percent of the success of their companies is attributable to marketplace positioning. If you agree that marketplace capital is most important and you acknowledge that you do not have it, then you are directed to your course: *"You've got to get it!"*

There are other new capital development systems. **Organizational capital development** is most critical among them. Organization capital is accomplished by the capacity to systematically and continuously align resources in your corporations with your marketplace positioning. Now let us ask:

How many of you believe that your corporations are continuously aligned with continuously changing marketplace positioning?

None? Your organizations grew like Topsy? You are stuck with a legacy of unchanging entities? Then you already know the answer to your projections of success. Organizational capital development is about continuously "rearchitecting" the organization. Either you have it or you don't!

What about **human capital development**? Do you use the adjectival modifiers *"human capital"* as seriously as they are intended? They are not just another set of terms for personnel or human resources! They mean empowering people to think generatively or innovatively to meet the requirements of organizational alignment. So we ask:

How many of you believe that your corporations are continuously empowering real human capital in interdependency with organizational capital?

Well, you tried to teach your people to relate interpersonally (soft skills) and perform technically (hard skills). You get an **"E"** for effort—not an **"I"** for intellect. Human capital development is about *"brainpower"* development. If you don't get it, you don't get it!

Now let us turn to an area that most people believe they know something about—**information capital development.** Information capital development is the information modeling required for human processing. Information models are multidimensional models that bring the phenomena that we are processing to life. Here we ask:

> How many of you believe that your corporations are continuously developing information capital in interdependency with human capital?

Sure, you have connectivity with your information systems. And you have communication due to this connectivity! But what do you communicate? The lowest levels of information capital—data and concepts about the relationships between data! While conceptual information does not prohibit human processing, it does retard it. So let us think of our current communication and knowledge management systems as *"depressor variables"* in the equation for enabling generative human processing. Information capital development is about information modeling. It involves pictures—lots of pictures! If you can't produce pictures, don't bother pretending to process generatively.

Finally, we turn to **mechanical capital development,** the continuous tooling and retooling of machine systems to be driven by information systems—the same systems that gave us the semiconductor chip and that now generate a spiraling array of products on land and sea and in the sky. So we ask:

> How many of you believe that your corporations are continuously developing mechanical capital in interdependency with information capital?

Well, you certainly have provided the mechanical underpinnings for our information connectivity. You also have produced an incredible array of mechanical products and services. Is it enough to muddle through to meet the spiraling requirements of the global marketplace? You already know the answer. It is no longer in control! Mechanical capital development is about continuous mechanical tooling. It must be driven by higher-order new capital development systems. Then it can, in turn, contribute to new directions.

Now we would like to ask:

> If all of these new capital development systems are so critical to the success of your organizations, then how come no one ever taught you about them?

Let us put that question in another way:

- Were you taught to systematically and continuously reposition your corporation so that you could co-orchestrate all of your partnered entities in a changing marketplace?

- Were you taught to systematically and continuously align your organization with continuously changing marketplace positioning so that you could generate interdependent cooperation within all of the units in a changing organization?

- Were you taught to systematically and continuously empower your people in thinking skills to implement changing organizational alignment, so that you could generate interdependent collaboration between all of the people?

- Were you taught to systematically and continuously model information in multidimensional forms to meet changing human-processing requirements, so that you could generate interdependent communication between all entities—people, units, organizations, markets?

- Were you taught to systematically and continuously tool and retool your machine systems as driven by information-systems requirements, so that you could provide the basic connectivity between all entities?

If your answer to any or all of these questions is *"No,"* then you know what you need to do. If your answer to all of these questions is *"Yes,"* then please contact us, for we have discovered a *"possibilities leader"* who can teach us a thing or two.

The *possibilities leader* is a person who can process interdependently and continuously with all phenomena—people, data, things. Such processing is achieved by:

- Utilizing **information relating systems** to transform conceptual information into operational information about phenomena;

- Utilizing **information representing systems** to transform operational information into dimensional information about phenomena;

- Utilizing **individual processing systems** to generate new images of phenomenal information;

- Utilizing **interpersonal processing systems** to generate more powerful images of phenomenal information;

- Utilizing **interdependent processing systems** to generate the most powerful images of phenomenal information.

The *possibilities leader* has an ever-expanding domain of influence. This influence proceeds, first and foremost, from his or her dedication to generating a *"possibilities organization"* through new capital development:

- **Marketplace capital development** for the co-orchestration of partners;

- **Organizational capital development** for the cooperation of units;

- **Human capital development** for the collaboration of people;

- **Information capital development** for the communication of models;

- **Mechanical capital development** for the connectivity of machines.

You can view the interrelationship of the leadership and organizational dimensions in Figure 1. As shown, the leadership systems culminate in interdependent processing: I^1, I^2, I^3, I^4, I^5. In turn, the organization systems are *nested* in marketplace capital development: MCD, OCD, HCD, ICD, mCD. Potentially all areas of leadership processing relate to all levels of new capital development (NCD), and vice versa. This means that I^5 generates NCD. In turn, NCD generates I^5. This means that I^5 leadership and NCD organization have an interdependent and synergistic, or growth-producing, relationship:

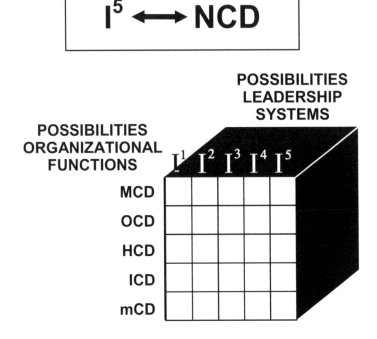

Figure 1. The Possibilities Management Paradigm

You can readily see that changes are indeed spiraling. Changes in the marketplace! In organizations! In people! In information! In tools! Indeed, you may conclude that all phenomena are inherently changeable.

To become *possibilities leaders*, you must align with these changes:

- **Relating** to them to discover their potential,
- **Empowering** them to enhance their potential,
- **Freeing** them to release their potential.

To accomplish this, you must acquire, apply, and transfer interdependent processing systems, thus generating new capital development in your organizations.

In summary:

> *Possibilities leaders* are about generating *possibilities organizations,* and vice versa: *possibilities organizations* generate *possibilities leadership.*

Culture change is clearly the issue of our time. Because we are not burdened by dysfunctional traditions, we can be shaped by future requirements—in this case, by the requirements of new capital development. In turn, we can shape the requirements for the global marketplace and the global community. The twenty-first century will yield a global marketplace and community that are interdependently related and interdependently generated by *possibilities leaders* and *possibilities organizations.*

Welcome To
A Special Kind of Book!

This is a book of pictures. We call the pictures *information models*. Information models are the universal language of processing in the twenty-first century. They are the interdependent and synergistic processing partners with human processors or human capital. We relate to phenomena, represent them, and then generate increasingly more powerful information models of the phenomena. That is the thesis of this book: interdependent processing generates prepotent models of phenomena. The reader need not conquer the processing operations involved: there is time for that later with different experiences and materials. The reader need only experience the magical images of any and all phenomena; to be introduced to the generation of powerful possibilities; to realize the accomplishments of generations of work in an afternoon of processing.

RRC and BGB

The equation for wealth is an evolving one. As marketplace requirements change, the capital ingredients change. Conventional wisdom aside, "capital" simply means what is "most important." Superstitious behavior to the contrary, financial capital is no longer "most important." Today, finances account for less than 15 percent of the variance in economic productivity growth. The emerging ingredients of new capital development account for more than 85 percent of growth.

I

Introduction and Overview

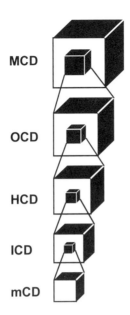

MCD

OCD

HCD

ICD

mCD

1 The Possibilities Economics

New capital development defines five new sources of wealth that define our organizations' requirements.

"It Was a Great Run . . ."
—A Case for Thought

The information-technology corporation was a very successful corporation. It had a 10-year track record of incessant growth in gross and profit. That growth was a direct outcome of the corporation's simple business formula, which looked like this:

- High-quality, low-cost positioning
- Sales-driven organization
- Aggressive sales force   **+ $ ⟶ Growth**
- Credible information support
- Standardized product-line

The formula, or equation, was put into practice as follows:

- First, the policymakers established "high-quality, low-cost" positioning to provide customers with *"big bang for the buck."* Competing in a marketplace with much costlier customized and even tailored software, it delivered maximum benefits for minimum price.

- Second, the organization was aligned with this positioning. This was a relatively flat, sales-driven organization. Basically, after initial product-development efforts, the organization was defined by two levels: a sales level, and a management level that supported the sales. The success of this organizational scheme led to unquestioned "functional autonomy" for the sales reps enabled by meeting sales quotas.

- Third, the sales force was composed of highly motivated salespeople. Aggressiveness was reinforced by two things: the company's unwritten sales credo—

7

"The optimum sale is one that the customer does not need and cannot use"—and an extraordinary commission system that made the retained salespeople well-to-do.

- Fourth, the organization did not require great technical expertise of its salespeople since it did not emphasize service. Instead, it supported them with credible "sales" information that created the illusion of expertise.

- Fifth and finally, the organization delivered a highly leveraged product-line. The line was technically powerful, including all of the innovations that could be found in the industry. While it developed some unique features, generally it was a more commercial version of the competition's research-and-development outputs. For this reason, the product-line could be priced as *"relatively inexpensive"* for its customers.

This was a great success story. It was a great run. Then, while everyone in the company was counting their earnings in cash and stock ownership, the world began to change. The market was being saturated with competitor products that cloned the company's capabilities. As prices were being driven downwards, the high-quality, low-cost market space was filling up with competition. Soon, the sales-driven organization began to look untenable. Sales quotas were getting too difficult to reach, and there was a hemorrhaging of salespeople to other companies. The remaining sales force, though aggressive, was now addressing customer requirements that were equally, if not more, aggressive. Customers who were not buying from the lowest-price providers were making their demands known: *"Our purchases are not based on 'best price' or 'best technology' anymore; they're based on 'culture change requirements.' We won't buy from you unless you can help us change our corporate cultures to adopt your products."* Frankly, the "credible" information that once had helped to make a sale was not good enough to service corporate culture change. Now, in light of these changing requirements, the product-lines looked awfully complicated for the benefits they delivered.

The company that had been positioned at the "razor's edge" of commerciality for so long was now falling, leaning headlong into commoditization and attenuation. What was going wrong? Could it save itself? Was its future, in all probability, already written? Could it be renewed, with new possibilities?

Today we are all participants in *"probabilities economics."* We participate in *probabilities economics* when we build our organizations to exploit the discoveries of the past, thinking that what worked yesterday will *probably* work today and tomorrow. The economics of probabilities, however, are the economics of time-limited commerciality followed by product and service commoditization and eventual attenuation. All organizations operate with the same available machinery, the same information, the same "best practices," and the same strategies for organizational networking; consequently, products and services become more and more undifferentiated.

The economic theories of probabilities do not adequately describe our changing present or future economic landscapes. To stay in business, we must proactively build our organizations to develop the evolving forces of our economy. We call our approach to these evolving forces *"possibilities economics."*

Possibilities economics builds upon historical sources of wealth generation and projects evolving and future sources. We begin constructing our model of such economics by tracing the evolutionary march of *"technological breakthroughs"* that have driven our economy. From the broadest perspective, economic growth in the marketplace and comparative advantage for organizations are driven by *"breakthroughs in technology development."* Agrarian technologies of seeding and herding were early *"breakthroughs,"* with agrarian methods and tools operating as sources of economic growth and comparative advantage. These technologies transformed the nomadic tribes of our hunter-gatherer ancestors into

9

farming communities of agricultural people. In a similar manner, industrial machinery and systems transformed farming communities into industrial organizations. As we will see in this book, new technologies are now changing our industrial organizations.

Relatedly, it is not until new *"breakthrough technologies"* are developed that the contributions of earlier technologies to wealth creation are fully realized, or *"capitalized."* For example, we did not actualize, or *"capitalize,"* the benefits of our agrarian technologies until we developed mechanical technologies to mechanize our agricultural practices. Similarly, we did not *"capitalize"* the productivity of our mechanical technologies until we developed information technologies to drive our machines. Likewise, we will not *"capitalize"* the potential of our information technologies until we develop human technologies to empower and free innovation. Moreover, we will not *"capitalize"* our human technologies until we develop organizational technologies to align our organizations. Finally, we will not *"capitalize"* the impact of organizational technologies until we have developed marketplace technologies to help us position our organizations in the marketplace.

MECHANICAL TECHNOLOGIES

The mechanical-technology marketplace is the market of machinery and the products and services delivered by machines. The comparative benefits of mechanical technologies peaked at the height of the Industrial Age, and have all but disappeared due to the standardization of mechanical operations. From this perspective, we may view the decline of mechanical technologies (mT) as a source of comparative advantage, or *"competitive edge,"* for organizations (see Figure 1-1).

Manufacturing processes typically rely on some form of the mechanical assembly line. All companies automate their machinery to the maximum. All install statistical process controls to maximize the quality of machine outputs. In short, everyone who is dedicated to being equal is becoming equal in the mechanical production of off-the-shelf products for customers.

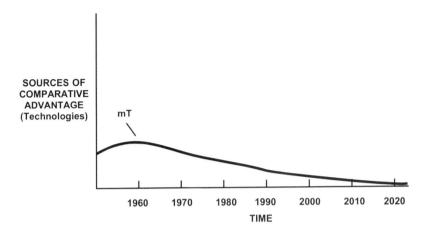

**Figure 1-1. Market Impact of
Mechanical Technologies (mT)**

By choosing to offer our customers products and services
through manufacturing processes, we are choosing to position ourselves in an attenuating market. Without *breakthroughs,* mechanical technologies will continue to decline as a source of comparative
advantage. Basically, this means a *level playing field* for everyone:
if we are willing to make the investment in machinery and information systems to drive our machines, we can compete for declining profits. This is not to say that the market for mechanical and
even agricultural products and services is not huge: it represents
several trillion dollars globally, and there is still much money to be
made. It is to say that many mechanical technologies have been
around since the Industrial Age and simply yield the *least competitive edge.*

Whether or not we choose to define our organizations as
mechanical operations, every organization is impacted by its ability
to manage mechanical technologies. At the production or delivery
levels, in particular, there is a great need to understand mechanical technologies and their applications.

An expanded vision of mechanical technologies will be introduced later in this book, in **Chapter 6, Managing Mechanical
Capital Development.** There you will learn how to construct a
model of mechanical capital development (mCD), one that

describes the processes used by mechanical capital to accomplish its goals or intentions. You will also learn about the following:

- The components, or parts, of mechanical capital and their definitions;

- How the components are related to machinery functions;

- The vectors, or forces, that act upon mechanical capital;

- How the vectors direct us to discover and apply new machinery by identifying what is needed and why it is needed;

- The managerial practices that are necessary for meeting mCD responsibilities.

The mCD process is one of the five sources of wealth generation that we have identified as critical for every organization to manage. The process allows us to start building our **New Capital Development (NCD) Equation for Wealth Generation,** a formula that is valid for the twenty-first century and beyond. With *breakthroughs* in mCD, the equation for wealth becomes redefined (see Figure 1-2).

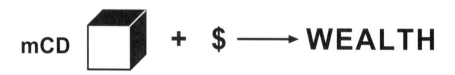

**Figure 1-2. Wealth Driven
by Mechanical Capital**

Mechanical capital development is its own source of wealth. In an economy empowered by mCD technologies, it is mechanical capital that drives the production of products and services in the marketplace.

INFORMATION TECHNOLOGIES

The information-technology marketplace is the market of information products and services. Themselves products of *breakthroughs* in electronics, information technologies (IT) climaxed as sources of comparative advantage in the 1980s. While driving our mechanical technologies to actualize their contributions, today's information technologies are also diminishing as a source of comparative advantage (see Figure 1-3). While their innovation potential remains infinite, their current comparative advantage is receding as the marketplace experiences the *"leveling"* effects of the near-instantaneous dissemination of information. Although the total size of the IT marketplace continues to grow, this dissemination has limited the competitive advantage of information technologies, since most companies now have access to reasonably priced, off-the-shelf and customized hardware and software, as well as a wide circulation of information.

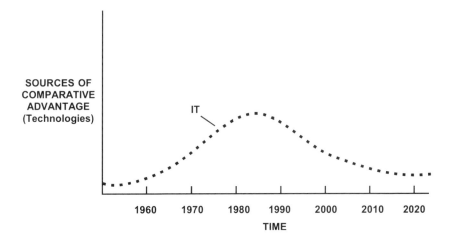

Figure 1-3. Market Impact of Information Technologies

By choosing to define our organizations as IT businesses, such as computer hardware, software, or publishing, we are choosing to position ourselves in a commoditizing market curve.

Current corporate interest in *"intellectual capital"* and *"knowledge management"* reflects a growing concern about identifying and exploiting information as a source of wealth creation and comparative advantage. Groupware connectivity, database mining, and report-generation software are examples of current efforts in this market for *"information capital."* However, these efforts focus upon information access, not information capital development. In other words, it is assumed that the present information in our systems is of *"capital"* value and that we just need to access it. In reality, the marketplace has a great void in its current understanding of how to define and create valuable *"information capital."*

More managers and employees are responsible for creating and managing more and better information today than at any other time in history. This is a trend that is here to stay. Whether or not we choose to define our organizations as providers of information products or services, every organization is impacted by its ability to manage the use of information technologies. More important, every organization is impacted by its ability to manage the development of new and valuable information capital.

Future mechanical *breakthroughs* in micro-electronics aside, IT companies will contribute to "growing" the trillion-dollar market only by more broadly and deeply defining and addressing the information-capital requirements of the marketplace.

Information capital development (ICD) methods and technologies will be introduced in **Chapter 5, Managing Information Capital Development.** In that chapter, you will learn the basics of ICD, including the following:

- Useful new ways to define and develop information capital (you will probably never look at a nugget of information in the same way again!);

- New methods for modeling ideas— ones that will help to accelerate our ideational processes;

- Managerial practices necessary for handling ICD processes.

Information capital development, a critical source of wealth generation for every organization, allows us to continue building our **NCD Equation for Wealth Generation.** As the computer and telecommunication industries further converge upon a common mission— "the unimpeded flow of global information"—the equation for wealth generation is continually redefined (see Figure 1-4).

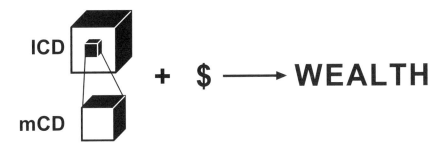

**Figure 1-4. Wealth Driven
by Information Capital**

In the evolving Age of Ideation, the generation of information capital development replaces information resources as a source of wealth and competitive advantage. Together, information capital development and mechanical capital development become interdependent and synergistic, with each continuously redefined by its contributions to generating wealth. In an economic system powered by ICD technologies, information capital emerges as a *driving* ingredient in the generation of wealth.

HUMAN TECHNOLOGIES

The human-technology marketplace is the market of products and services that support and enable human capital development (HCD). Thus far, our economies have focused upon mechanical and information technologies, and have grown in imbalance with our efforts to develop our human resources. Human technologies (HT) are an emerging source of growth and comparative advantage (see Figure 1-5).

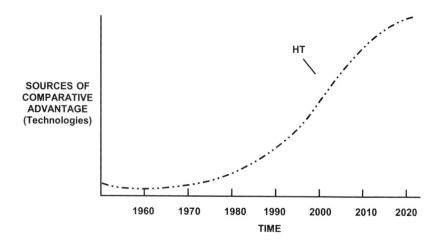

**Figure 1-5. Market Impact of
Human Technologies (HT)**

The markets of human resource development, or education and training, represent more than one-half trillion dollars in the United States and are growing at the rate of nearly 10 percent per year. Although these huge markets are half the size of the trillion-dollar IT marketplace, we must remember one thing: it is *human performance* that develops information and mechanical products and services. Until we actualize the generative and innovative capabilities of our human capital, we will not actualize the potential contributions of information or machinery for wealth creation.

The business sector's growing interest in *"human capital"* and *"core competencies"* testifies to an increasing need to understand the ingredients of effective human performance. For businesses today, the HCD marketplace strategies are a mix of technical training and "soft-skills" training. "Soft skills" are identifiable as multiple variations of basic interpersonal-communication skills. Generally, these skills are considered today's current *"human technologies."* However, the future skills requirements for human capital development are primarily intellectual skills that empower generativity and innovativeness.

By choosing to define our organizations as human-technology businesses, and offering education, training, consulting services, or

16

related software or media products, we are choosing to position ourselves in a now-accelerating commercial market curve. Requirements to elevate human performance have created a growth market. With an increased understanding of the factors that leverage human performance, companies will grow this HCD marketplace, empowering more and more people as sources of comparative advantage. It is critical that we understand and apply a new set of human technologies — methods to develop generative and innovative human performers.

Whether or not we choose to define our organizations as providers of HCD products or services, every organization is impacted by its ability to define and apply human technologies. Most important, every organization is impacted by its ability to empower and support innovative human performance. Employees who can think are of growing value. Managers and employees at every organizational level have a great need to understand and apply human technologies for human capital development.

New human technologies to empower innovation will be introduced in **Chapter 4, Managing Human Capital Development.** There we will focus on how to model the critical operations of HCD: the skills that thinking people need, the organizational responsibilities involved, and the critical information processes required to service these organizational functions. We will also take a look at the following:

- New ways to measure human performance—ways that will make an impact on how we view employee selection, performance management, and education and training;

- Identifying new areas of performance that are personally interesting;

- Managerial practices necessary for managing HCD effectively.

HCD technologies and methods are a crucial source of wealth generation for us and our organizations. With them, we may further build our **NCD Equation for Wealth Generation.** As *breakthroughs* in human technologies occur, the equation continues to be redefined (see Figure 1-6).

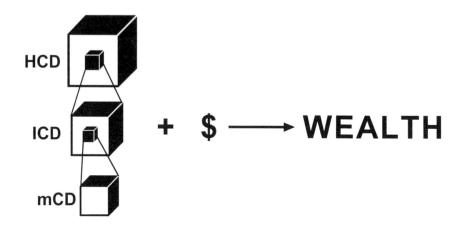

**Figure 1-6. Wealth Driven
by Human Capital**

In the evolving Age of Ideation, human resources are redefined as innovative human processors, or human capital. Together, human capital development, information capital development, and mechanical capital development become interdependent and synergistic: each is continuously redefined by its contributions to generating wealth.

In an economic system powered by HCD technologies, human capital emerges as a *driving* economic ingredient. In synergistic relationship with information capital, human capital is capable of creating entirely new ingredients of wealth generation.

ORGANIZATIONAL TECHNOLOGIES

The organizational-technology marketplace is the market for organizational architecture and alignment services and support products. Organizational technologies (OT) are another emerging source of growth and comparative advantage, as we can clearly see in Figure 1-7.

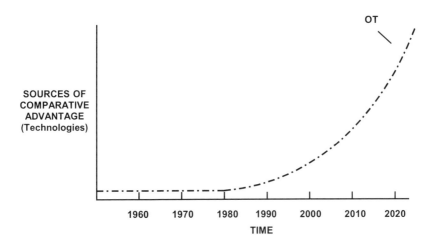

**Figure 1-7. Market Impact of
Organizational Technologies (OT)**

With the "information overload" produced by information technologies, we decentralized our corporate operations. The effects
were two-edged. On the one hand, decentralization allowed new
sources of growth to emerge naturalistically—primary among
them, human and information sources. On the other hand, decentralization dismantled the organization as a powerful source of
effect in its own right.

We may realize that all of our resources—including machines,
information, and people—operate within the contexts of our
organizations; yet, until we actualize the functional alignment of
our organizations' operations, we will not actualize these wealth-
generating resources.

The need for continuous organizational alignment, within and
between organizations, is ubiquitous. It is estimated that we are
already spending 5 percent of GDP on internal restructuring annu-
ally: this would put the market estimate in the United States at
over one-quarter trillion dollars and growing. In a changeable
marketplace, every viable organization will engage in continuous
organizational alignment throughout the twenty-first century. The
commercial market for organizational alignment services and
support products is a growth market.

Recent corporate interest in the *"reengineering"* of processes and the *"quality function deployment" (QFD)* of resources — as well as in *"self-organizing systems"* and *"flat," "matrixed," "virtual,"* and *"learning"* organizations — reflects a recognition that the organization itself requires attention as a valuable source of effect. The idea of the organization as a *"productive agency"* has reemerged. However, the aforementioned strategies of organizational architecture have already "played out." Corporate consultants and executives are now asking, "What's next?"

The market requires that organizational technologies serve both internal and external alignment. Organizational methodologies are needed for the internal alignment of all of the organization's critical operations: its goals or intentions, its resources, and its processes. Organizational technologies also need to deliver operational processes for external alignment with suppliers, vendors, and customer organizations.

New organizational-alignment technologies will be introduced in **Chapter 3, Managing Organizational Capital Development.** There you will learn about all of the following:

- Effective ways to use multidimensional modeling systems to describe how organizations work;

- How to diagnose organizational operations by measuring the presence or absence of critical operations;

- The importance of organizational information flows — deductive, inductive, and idiosyncratic;

- New ways to measure organizational performance — ways that will make an impact on your view of reengineering, restructuring, and realigning organizations;

- Managerial practices necessary for managing organizational capital development (OCD).

OCD, a critical source of wealth for every organization, allows us to build on our **NCD Equation for Wealth Generation** for the twenty-first century. With *breakthroughs* in organizational technologies, our equation is further refined to include the impact of OCD technologies (see Figure 1-8).

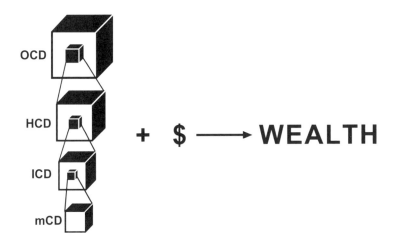

Figure 1-8. Wealth Driven by Organizational Capital

OCD technologies revitalize the organization by aligning the organization internally: its goals, resources, and processes. OCD technologies revitalize the organization with external-alignment strategies to align with suppliers and vendors as well as customers. This alignment defines organizational capital and results in the increased efficiency and effectiveness of what we call a *"possibilities organization."*

MARKETPLACE TECHNOLOGIES

Every organization is involved in making decisions about marketplace positioning and partnering. The market for positioning services to assist in these responsibilities is the market for marketplace technologies. Marketplace-positioning and -partnering methodologies enable producer organizations to strategically analyze and address their own marketplace requirements and values. These same technologies are also used to analyze the requirements and values of customers and competitors. Marketplace technologies (MT) are the most powerful source of continuous growth and comparative advantage (see Figure 1-9).

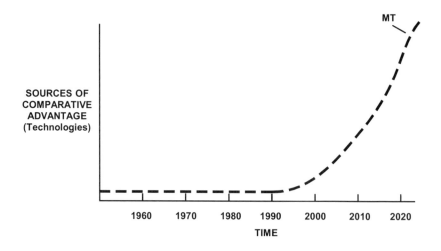

**Figure 1-9. Market Impact of
Marketplace Technologies (MT)**

Most of us have already conceded that marketplace positioning is the prepotent source of corporate success. This, our greatest and most urgent corporate need, makes the marketplace-technology market a growth market.

Marketplace positioning is about positioning an organization in relation to other businesses in the marketplace. It implies aligning organizational divisions and units, positioning the talents of employees, positioning technologies, machinery, processes, and products and services, all in relation to counterparts in the economic marketplace.

Today, marketplace-positioning practices revolve around a few simple yet profound interrogatives:

- *"What business are you in?"*

- *"What business would you like to be in?"*

- *"How do you think you can make the transition?"*

- *"What are the obstacles?"*

Our current tools for marketplace positioning include market research, trend analysis, "what-if" scenario development, financial analyses, and industry best-practices benchmarking.

Requirements are imposed upon marketplace-positioning methods and practices: they must serve the policymaker's responsibilities regarding strategic decision-making and mergers and acquisitions; they must assist in making decisions about whether to enter a new market niche and whether to sell off a business line. Marketplace-positioning technologies can be defined as the *"how-to"* processes of marketplace positioning. Specifically, these technologies must help policymakers represent the values and capabilities of organizations and relate them to the requirements and opportunities of the marketplace. These technologies must walk policymakers through processes for positioning their organizations. With this in mind, we must ask ourselves whether our current marketplace-positioning strategies are adequate for the requirements of positioning our businesses for the next century.

New marketplace-positioning technologies will be introduced in **Chapter 2, Managing Marketplace Capital Development.** There we will focus on the following:

- New, useful ways to analyze the marketplace positioning of an organization;

- Methods for measuring the requirements of the marketplace;

- Methods for measuring the values and capabilities of the marketplace of organizations in response to those requirements;

- How to position organizations in the marketplace of organizations;

- Managerial practices necessary for managing marketplace capital development (MCD).

By the time you finish reading Chapter 2, you will look at your organization's marketplace positioning quite differently than you did before! You will have learned new ways to measure marketplace positioning, and this will surely make an impact on how you view partnering and future mergers and acquisitions.

MCD is a critical source of wealth for every organization. With the inclusion of MCD and marketplace technologies, our **NCD**

Equation for Wealth Generation assumes a comprehensive form. The equation is further expanded to incorporate MCD technologies (see Figure 1-10).

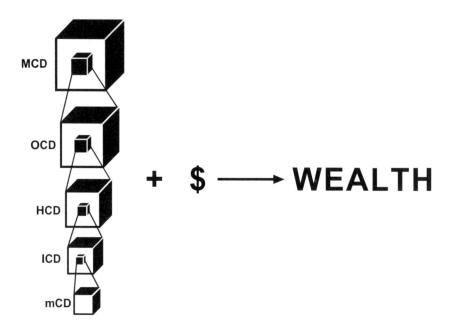

**Figure 1-10. Wealth Driven by
Marketplace Capital**

Policymakers are continuously processing the positioning of their organizations to maximize meeting and exceeding both current and future marketplace requirements.

NCD EQUATION FOR WEALTH GENERATION

In our **NCD Equation for Wealth Generation** (shown in Figure 1-11), financial capital is reduced to a catalytic ingredient— necessary but not sufficient for capital development.

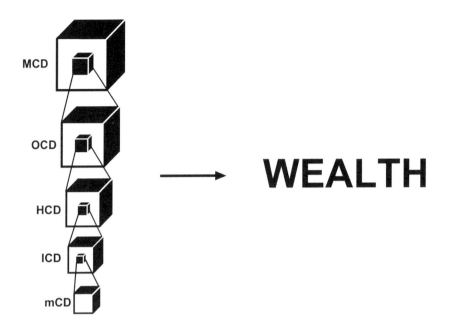

**Figure 1-11. NCD Equation for
Wealth Generation**

As accounting procedures for *keeping score,* finances may appear on
either side of the equation. Finances are used to invest in capital
resource development and are used to measure the value of the
many criteria of wealth. The new reality of ever-expanding wealth
is generated by the ingredients of new capital development.

II

New Capital Development— The Possibilities Management System

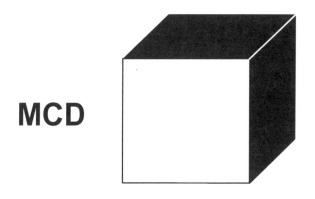

MCD

2 Managing Marketplace Capital Development

Positioning in the marketplace is the context for wealth generation.

"A Contrast of Extremes . . ."
—The Power of Positioning

Attempting to anticipate future requirements in their marketplace, Companies A and B met for a series of discussions. These discussions between the two competitors centered on joint venturing to build the world's *"cutting-edge"* product. Utilizing the exact same market data, the companies positioned themselves differentially in the marketplace: Company A decided to continue on its current course and customize its standard product-line; Company B decided to *"go it alone"* in an attempt to tailor future product-lines to marketplace requirements. The implications of this differential positioning would be profound.

First of all, differential positioning in relation to the exact same market requirements means differences in values: differential positioning is a function of the interaction of values with requirements; power-positioning is an attempt to maximize meeting both values and requirements.

In this context, Company A's value system revolves around conservative, probabilistic principles: stick to what we do best and avoid taking risks.

In turn, Company B's value system revolves around progressive, possibilistic principles: reach for what we can do best and take the risks.

Moreover, both companies are differentiated in their corporate capacities, reflecting their values:

- Company A is committed to maximizing the contributions of its powerful, existing technologies—mechanical and information technologies.

33

- Company B is committed to developing new corporate capacities to accomplish its initiative positioning— human, organizational, and marketplace technologies to drive its information and mechanical technologies.

Their marketplace positioning established, the leaders of Company A have spelled out a policy of incrementalism to deal with production bottlenecks and declining profits. The broad outlines of the plan include modernizing the computer systems, trimming thousands of jobs, and remaking relationships with the company's huge supply chain.

A redesign of assembly operations has actually been underway for several years. However, at one point it got detoured by a big production push to compete with arch-rival, Company B. Company A won the competition, but the effort sent costs spiraling and profits down. In addition, global economic problems have had an impact on Company A, leaving many orders unfilled.

However, Company A has a lot more going for it than meets the eye on the profit sheet. It has historic positioning as the premier builder of products. Moreover, it has futuristic positioning as the exclusive builder of some products, for example, those from its defense division. Company A has already acquired companies that enable it to have proprietary technologies; these give it a competitive edge in bidding on large defense contracts.

Company B, in turn, is positioned to become the standard-setter in the marketplace. This means that it must bring to bear not only *"cutting-edge"* mechanical and information technologies, but also *"state-of-the-art"* human, organizational, and mechanical technologies; moreover, it must integrate the applications of all of these technologies.

Here we have a direct contrast of the extremes of marketplace positioning: one company dedicated historically to the potentially infinite variations of legacy learning; the other company dedicated futuristically to the potentially infinite variations of generative and innovative processing. Both compete on the same playing field: one with a conservative and stable game plan; the other with a continuous interdependent processing system.

The management of marketplace positioning projects the business and its enterprise networks in the marketplace. Positioning is futuristic in orientation. Managing marketplace positioning emphasizes preparing as-yet-unborn generations of business opportunities for continuous repositioning in the marketplace. We label the process of continuous marketplace positioning "marketplace capital development," or "MCD."

Of course, many other forms of new capital development are directed by this positioning.

- When Company A and its new acquisitions integrate and elevate organizational relationships aligned with marketplace positioning, we say that they have developed *organizational capital.*

- When the people of both organizations are related and empowered to generate business innovations and solutions, we say that they have developed *human capital.*

- When they incorporate new information-modeling technologies and concurrent planning for prototyping new designs, we say that they have developed *information capital.*

- Finally, when they incorporate new information-systems-driven mechanical technologies, such as "*augmented reality*" tools to track continuously changing wiring diagrams and parts lists, we say that they have developed *mechanical capital.*

All forms of new capital development flow deductively from marketplace capital. The organizational capital is aligned with positioning. The human capital is empowered for implementation. The information capital is modeled to partner with humans in processing. The mechanical capital is partnered with information in tooling.

Of course, the best positionings in the market are those not yet taken:

- Partnered constellation positioning with producers, suppliers, and vendors to develop marketplace capital in the changing marketplace;

- Relationship-driven marketing that actually empowers customer organizations to develop organizational capital;

- Empowering human processing systems that actually empower people to process interdependently as human capital;

- Information modeling systems that actually yield information capital which can be processed systematically with human capital;

- Mechanical tooling systems that implement information-systems-driven mechanical capital.

These positionings truly differentiate the corporation or product in the marketplace. They empower the organization and its partners and customers with new capital development. They underscore that the most powerful positioning is substantive positioning: positioning that we can really deliver; positioning that we can follow through upon; positioning that we can build upon for ourselves and our friends.

Possibilities organizations begin with positioning. Without positioning, the organization cannot gain and maintain comparative advantage over other organizations in the marketplace. Another way of saying this is that positioning differentiates our organization's contributions.

However, in today's world, we cannot talk about positioning as simply differentiating ourselves from our competitors. Competition is the function of independence. Independence and competition, as we once practiced it, will not work anymore. Today, we position as interdependent partnerships with nearly everyone: customers, customers of customers, vendors, suppliers, and, yes, even entities that we might still consider *"competitors."* Collaboration is the function of interdependence. Today, positioning differentiates our interdependent collaborative contributions.

All business policymakers will concede that the success of a corporation begins with its positioning in the marketplace. Yet all of these top executives also will admit that they were never taught *"positioning."* Many employ *"legacy positioning"* by "sticking to knitting" and adding new related product- and service-lines. Others employ *"existential positioning"* by "cleaning the slate" and entering those markets with highly leveraged opportunities. There are many other strategies in between these extremes—some very personal and idiosyncratic. But none are systematic in positioning their corporations in the marketplace!

One of the great ironies of business is that we know so much about the technologies we employ to produce our product- and service-lines, but so little about the technologies of the business practices that determine the success or failure of our businesses. That is partly the reason why our business successes are random and seldom replicated.

Increasingly, top executives are driven by fast-changing marketplace requirements. As *breakthroughs* evolve through the rapid market life-cycle, executives must address the derivative requirements of these *breakthroughs*. Marketplace requirements are not simply based upon corporate values or executive choices. The marketplace itself "speaks" and its requirements must be understood. With this understanding, corporations take an index of their capacities to address these requirements. Corporations need technological capabilities in precisely the same areas as the requirements.

To enable the corporation to mobilize its technological capacities to address its marketplace requirements, executives must understand the processes of marketplace positioning. All positioning to enhance corporate capacities to meet marketplace requirements is accompanied by implications for placement in the life-cycle of the market.

We must remember: no organization is an independent entity. Our organizations are inextricably linked in the market's life-cycle, from generativity and innovation through commercialization to commoditization and attenuation. Marketplace positioning must relate customer requirements with producer technologies, all within the context of the market's life-cycle.

Three points are particularly important here:

- First, understanding the requirements of the marketplace is crucial to positioning. In effect, marketplace requirements are the values of the marketplace. This is analogous to career placement: we have our values, and the job has its own values; the values of the job become the requirements of the person. In marketplace positioning, the marketplace values become the organization's requirements. Our *external mission* is to position our organizations to meet or to exceed these marketplace requirements.

- Second, gaining the technological capability to meet marketplace requirements is our *internal mission*. This, too, is analogous to career placement: if we have the right skills, knowledge, and attitudes, we can get the job. Mobilizing technological capacity to meet marketplace requirements is the essential function of the organization.

- Third, how we address the requirements of the marketplace with our corporate capacities has implications for our placement in the market life-cycle. Beginning with generativity, possibilities are transformed into marketplace applications by innovation, and culminate in profitable products and services by commercialization. An interdependent partnering relationship among these three phases of the market life-cycle is essential for powerful positioning in the marketplace.

Technological capabilities and marketplace requirements are both "moving targets" in the market life-cycle. Whatever organization *best understands the market's requirements, builds its technological capabilities,* and *partners across the market life-cycle* is taking the first step toward becoming a ***"possibilities organization."***

Although generic marketplace-positioning strategies can be taught and learned, all applications of positioning are unique. In this respect, our own experience is worthy. We have three companies: a consulting and training company, a publishing company, and a research and development company. We positioned and empowered both our consulting-training and publishing companies to address the market's human resource development (HRD) requirements. Essentially, we mobilized our HRD technological capacities to address HRD marketplace requirements. Initially, our HRD technologies placed these companies in the innovative phase of the market life-cycle. Over time, with widespread adoption of HRD requirements and HRD technologies, this positioning moved us to the commercial phase of the market life-cycle.

Today, HRD market requirements and technological capacities are changing. With *breakthroughs* in human capital development (HCD), our consulting-training and publishing companies are entering the commoditization phase of the HRD market life-cycle. While corporate positioning may stand still, the market moves on. Consequently, to grow, both our businesses are required to reposition themselves in the marketplace.

Our R and D company is a generator of HCD technologies. Despite its many breakthroughs, the company alone is not positioned to capitalize on its research and development. It is the potential interdependent partnership between the generative R and D company and the commoditized consulting-training and publishing companies that promises to once again move the positioning of our organizations toward the innovative end of the market life-cycle. Ultimately, it is the interdependent relationship across generative, innovative, and commercial market phases that yields an enduring business enterprise.

MODELING MARKETPLACE POSITIONING

We define marketplace positioning as the relationship of corporate capabilities to marketplace requirements within the life-cycle of the market. Corporate capabilities may be defined in terms of corporate technologies—the methodologies that organizations have incorporated into their business, whether or not these methodologies are for sale directly. In turn, marketplace requirements are defined by customers. Marketplace requirements are the *"capital,"* or *"most important,"* products, services, solutions, and relationships—the ones that customers deem necessary to ensure their own successful performance in the marketplace. The market's life-cycle is defined and measured by levels of growth in gross and profitability and market penetration. Our positioning in the marketplace is defined by the relationship between our corporate technologies and the *"capital"* requirements of our customers within the market life-cycle.

Equipped with the information above, we can develop an operational model for representing marketplace requirements. We label our model "MCD," or "marketplace capital development." Building it involves four general steps:

1. Scaling the functions or requirements of marketplace positioning;

2. Scaling the components or capabilities that are representative of the technologies available to service marketplace requirements;

3. Scaling the market life-cycle of these functional requirements and corporate technologies;

4. Representing the interaction of these elements of MCD in a three-dimensional way.

This chapter will provide a demonstration of how to carry out these steps.

We manage our marketplace-positioning responsibilities by using our scaled MCD marketplace-positioning information. We cross our requirements and capabilities scales to develop matrices of marketplace-positioning information. By bringing these into interaction with the third scale, the market life-cycle scale, we develop a three-dimensional model of marketplace-positioning information. These scales, matrices, and models provide us with useful material for analyzing our current and future marketplace positioning.

Our model building will help us answer several critical questions to define our organizations' marketplace positioning. Those questions include:

- *Where are we now positioned...*
  - in relation to market requirements?
  - in relation to technological capabilities?
  - with our known (and previously defined) competitors?
  - with partners?
  - with customers?

- *Where do we want or need to reposition our organizations...*
  - in relation to market requirements?
  - in relation to technological capabilities?
  - with potential partners?
  - with future customers?

The growth or death of our organizations begins with how we model and manage marketplace positioning.

Scaling Marketplace Requirements

We begin modeling our marketplace positioning by scaling the requirements of the marketplace. A useful generic description of the functions or requirements of the marketplace is found in the analysis of new capital development (NCD) economic factors shown in Figure 2-1. We will take a closer look at each of these NCD market requirements in the course of this book.

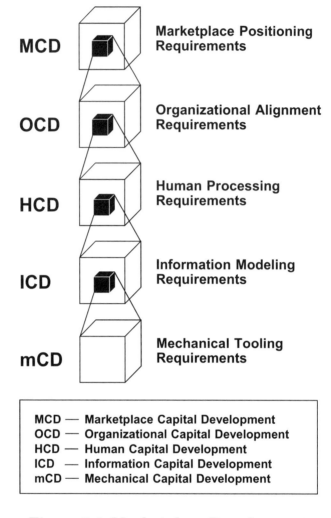

**Figure 2-1. Marketplace Requirements
in New Capital Development**

Figure 2-1 allows us to see the marketplace requirements as NCD requirements; it also shows us how the requirements are related. We may note the following:

- Mechanical capital development (mCD) requirements are driven by information capital development (ICD) requirements;

- Information capital development (ICD) requirements are driven by human capital development (HCD) requirements;

- Human capital development (HCD) requirements are driven by organizational capital development (OCD) requirements;

- Organizational capital development (OCD) requirements are driven by marketplace capital development (MCD) requirements.

Our analyses of the marketplace requirements begin with the evolving need for new capital development, or NCD, in all forms.

This table of marketplace requirements is a *"map-in"* to initial marketplace requirements. Further analyses of each type of capital development will provide a clearer description of the specific market requirements that we need to measure. Each set of NCD requirements is a subset of this generic scale of NCD marketplace requirements. As we learn more about how to model and manage each of these NCD sources of wealth, we will discover many useful *nested* market requirements—scales to aid us in our marketplace-positioning responsibilities.

If we want to stay in business, we have no choice but to respond to marketplace requirements. Once we have defined those requirements, the only remaining question is "How will we respond to meet the requirements?" Many organizations will respond, and a few exemplary ones— *"possibilities organizations"*—will even exceed the responses required and actually generate new requirements.

Scaling Corporate Capacities

Corporate capacities are needed to satisfy the capital-development requirements of the marketplace. Corporate capacities are defined as technologies that are used to fulfill market requirements (see Figure 2-2). We define corporate capacities by NCD technologies to address NCD requirements.

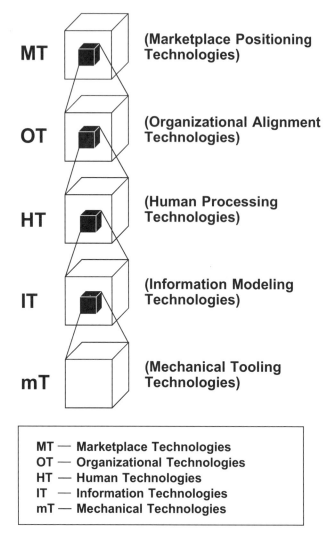

MT   **(Marketplace Positioning Technologies)**

OT   **(Organizational Alignment Technologies)**

HT   **(Human Processing Technologies)**

IT   **(Information Modeling Technologies)**

mT   **(Mechanical Tooling Technologies)**

MT — **Marketplace Technologies**
OT — **Organizational Technologies**
HT — **Human Technologies**
IT   — **Information Technologies**
mT — **Mechanical Technologies**

**Figure 2-2. Corporate Capacities
in New Capital Development Technologies**

Our scale of corporate capacities, presented in Figure 2-2, is comprehensive. All corporate capabilities can be modeled as capital-development technologies. This is a useful initial *map-in* to corporate technologies. Further analyses of corporate technologies will provide a clearer description of the technology capacities that we need to measure. For example, Chapter 5, which focuses on ICD, will provide more detailed scales for analyzing information-modeling technologies. These descriptions are subsets of the "Information Technologies" segment of the scale above. We will learn more about how we define each of these five areas of technological capacities. Then, we will apply these scales to measure our current capabilities and to orient ourselves toward technological capabilities for the future.

Marketplace Capital Matrix

When we model our scale of corporate capacities dedicated to accomplishing marketplace requirements, we create a basic matrix of marketplace capital, as shown in Table 2-1. As may be noted, potentially any or all corporate technologies may be dedicated to any or all marketplace requirements. For our purposes, the corporation's technological capacities are the components of the matrix. They are dedicated to the capital-development market requirements or functions.

Table 2-1. Marketplace Capital Matrix

MARKETPLACE REQUIREMENTS	CORPORATE CAPACITIES				
	MT	OT	HT	IT	mT
MCD					
OCD					
HCD					
ICD					
mCD					

We may use this matrix to represent the marketplace positioning of our organizations. The matrix helps us formulate initial questions about our positioning, which we may follow with more penetrating questions about marketplace requirements and the

45

nature of our technological capacities. It is with this initial matrix that we begin to see where our organization currently does business and where it does not. This analysis of requirements and capabilities should stimulate many important questions—questions whose answers may have an impact on our visions of what our organizations could become.

With the Marketplace Capital Matrix, we begin to position our organizations, and so develop the *marketplace capital* our organizations require.

Scaling the Market Life-Cycle

The ability of corporate capacities to achieve marketplace requirements are dependent upon placement in the market life-cycle (see Figure 2-3).

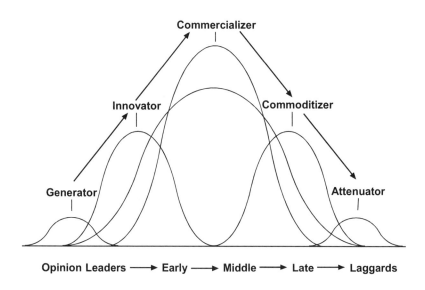

Figure 2-3. Phases of the Market Life-Cycle

The market life-cycle is most familiar to us in the so-called *adoption curve*. In the adoption curve, opinion leaders stimulate early interest, followed by early, middle, and late adopters, and finally, laggards. The bulk of the market falls with the middle adopters. We conceive of the sources of market adoption as the source of the market life-cycle:

- **Generators (G)** create the market with *breakthroughs* through R and D investments.

- **Innovators (I)** apply the *breakthroughs* in customer contexts with initial returns.

- **Commercializers (C)** expand contextual applications and commercialize the market.

- **Commoditizers (C′)** commoditize the market with diminishing profits.

- **Attenuators (A)** exploit the final phase of market acceptance with diminishing returns.

This market life-cycle applies to the evolution of all *technological breakthroughs* and so all products and services. We may represent the life-cycle in a simple scale, as shown in Table 2-2.

Table 2-2. Market Life-Cycle

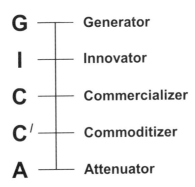

G	Generator
I	Innovator
C	Commercializer
C′	Commoditizer
A	Attenuator

The prepotent issue for twenty-first-century corporate leaders is this: *"How do we empower and accelerate our corporations to become drivers, rather than riders, in the marketplace?"* The short answer is simple: interdependency—with generators, innovators, and commercializers. The implementation of this relationship

releases the power of the marketplace into the policy of the corporation.

In the market life-cycle, the generators are initially outside the
adoption curve and their products are brought into the curve by the
innovators. The generators are interdependently related to their
substance and, usually, only tangentially related to the market.
The innovators, in turn, are oriented to the application of *breakthroughs* in the context of customer concerns.

The *"gaps"* between the products of generators and innovators
are large, while those between innovators and the commercial
marketplace are enormous. In the final analysis, such *"gaps"*
within the middle-adopter marketplace can be *"bridged"* only by
commercializers, who themselves are interdependently related to
the market's visions of its wants and needs. The commercializers'
functions are the most complex of all: to be interdependent with
both market and technologies. Commoditization occurs when the
commercializers have lost their relationships with either or both
the marketplace and their technologies. Attenuation soon follows.

In *marketplace capital development,* we position our organizations by forming interdependent relationships across the phases of
the market life-cycle. To ensure their corporation is dedicated to
growth, the commercializers relate interdependently with generators, who are able to create markets, and with innovators, who are
able to make applications and thus to initiate the market's movement.

Dimensionalizing the MCD Model

We complete our MCD model by adding the dimension of the
market life-cycle (see Figure 2-4). The objective of the MCD model
may be succinctly expressed as follows:

> *Marketplace requirements are discharged by
> corporate capabilities enabled by market-life-cycle
> placement.*

48

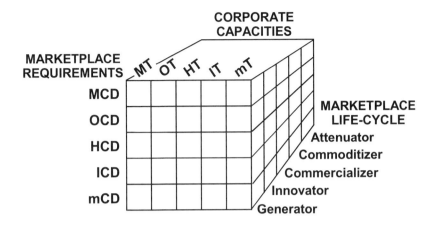

Figure 2-4. MCD Model

Marketplace positioning begins when we map our organizations into the MCD model. Once we have modeled our current positioning, we may model our future positioning. Only then can we orient our organizations toward alignment that fulfills our intended marketplace positioning.

Next we will focus upon processes that enable us to model and manage the positioning of our corporations in the marketplace—to model and manage our *marketplace capital*.

PROCESSES FOR MARKETPLACE POSITIONING

The MCD processes for marketplace positioning involve five phases:

Phase 1: **Requiring** for measuring marketplace requirements and opportunities;

Phase 2: **Valuing** for measuring corporate capabilities or capacities in relation to marketplace requirements and opportunities;

Phase 3: **Visioning** for discriminating our present and future positioning in relation to marketplace requirements (or opportunities) and corporate capabilities within the context of the market life-cycle;

Phase 4: **External Missioning** for communicating our "external" marketplace positioning;

Phase 5: **Internal Modeling** for communicating our "internal" marketplace-positioning policies.

To explain these processes for marketplace positioning, we will employ the example of a company with whom we, the authors, once worked. The company is in the information technology (IT) business; specifically, it is a provider of software for manufacturing design. Our goal was to help its leaders position the company in the marketplace.

Phase 1—Requiring

We initiated the **Requiring** phase of marketplace positioning by *mapping-in* our customer's intentions to meet the information capital development (ICD) requirements of the marketplace (see Table 2-3).

Table 2-3. Positioning on the Scale of Marketplace Requirements

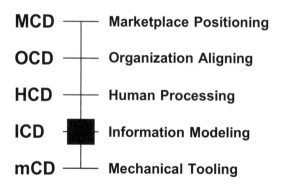

MCD	**Marketplace Positioning**
OCD	**Organization Aligning**
HCD	**Human Processing**
ICD	**Information Modeling**
mCD	**Mechanical Tooling**

The company leaders were well aware of spiraling ICD requirements, yet they acknowledged that the company had not yet been
able to articulate the dimensions of ICD; therefore, proactive positioning to meet these requirements was problematic. We helped
the leaders define the dimensions of ICD, and so define the market's current and evolving requirements for information modeling.
(More about the evolving requirements of the ICD market will be
presented in Chapter 5, Managing Information Capital Development.)

Phase 2—Valuing

We continued on to the **Valuing** phase. We helped the leaders
define their company's values in terms of current and future
technological capabilities; this expanded their understanding of
evolving ICD technologies. Next, we *mapped-in* our IT customer's
technological capabilities in relation to ICD requirements (see
Table 2-4).

**Table 2-4. Current Positioning in the
Marketplace Capital Matrix**

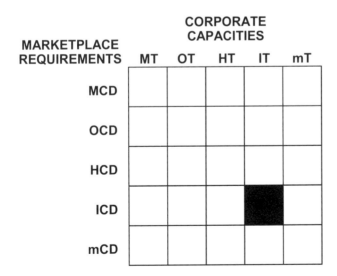

MARKETPLACE REQUIREMENTS	CORPORATE CAPACITIES				
	MT	OT	HT	IT	mT
MCD					
OCD					
HCD					
ICD				■	
mCD					

The customer had good capabilities in IT technologies and wanted to "stick to knitting." However, now equipped with an expanded understanding of evolving market requirements and technological capabilities, the leaders could see there was a great discrepancy between the company's current IT positioning and the marketplace's comprehensive requirements for ICD software— providing customers with software to comprehensively model and manage information capital development (see Table 2-5).

**Table 2-5. Future Positioning in the
Marketplace Capital Matrix**

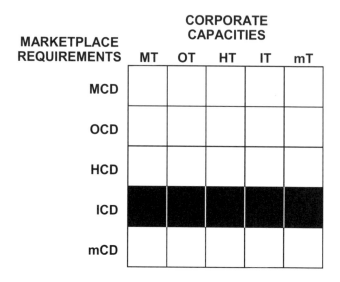

Accordingly, the leaders expanded their values, emphasizing the need to incorporate new technological capacities to service the ICD needs of their customers.

Phase 3—Visioning

In this phase of our work with the company's leaders, we developed a vision of current and future positioning using the MCD model, shown in Figure 2-5. As may be noted, we *mapped-in* our customer's market-life-cycle placement to complete an image of its current marketplace positioning. That image may be expressed as follows:

ICD requirements are discharged by IT capabilities enabled by market-life-cycle positioning as a marketplace commoditizer.

Consequently, not only was the company's IT positioning discrepant from what was needed to fully meet corporate values and marketplace requirements, but the company had lost its original generative and innovative, and then commercial, market positions.

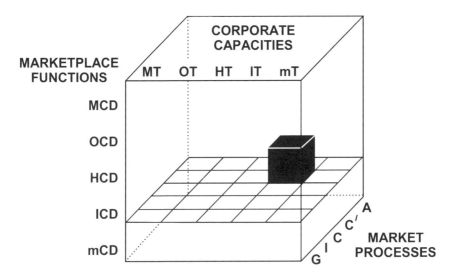

Figure 2-5. Current Positioning in the MCD Model

At this point, it was clear the company had to do more than develop information technologies for information modeling. To more comprehensively meet the market's ICD requirements and recover some of its former "front-end" positioning, the company needed to develop minimum levels of in-house capacity in several *additional* critical technologies: marketplace technologies for marketplace positioning, organizational technologies for organizational alignment, human technologies for human processing, and mechanical technologies for mechanical tooling (see Figure 2-6).

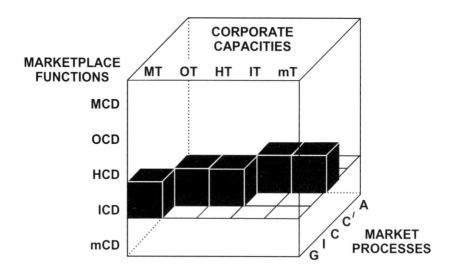

Figure 2-6. Future Positioning in the MCD Model

Furthermore, for the company to meet and *exceed* the ICD requirements of the marketplace, its corporate vision would have to emphasize continuous movement toward a new corporate positioning:

> *ICD market requirements discharged by capacitating technologies (ICD as well as MCD, OCD, HCD, and mCD) and enabled by new market partnerships to move closer to the generative and innovative end of the market life-cycle.*

Phase 4—External Missioning

In external missioning, we transform the positioning vision into an external mission: goals, targets, strategies. As we can see in Figure 2-7, the product and service goals were elevated from IT to ICD, with the support-services goals expanded to incorporate new capital development (NCD) technologies (MCD, OCD, HCD, ICD, and mCD). The company is now repositioning its external mission by adding marketplace-partnership consulting, organizational consulting, human-performance training services, and mechanical-product partnership reselling to its ICD/IT customer targets. In addition, it has redefined its strategic positioning from commoditization to partnering within the full range of market life-cycle representatives, from generators through attenuators. As illustrated, the strategies that the company employs to accomplish this positioning are as follows: leadership that generates mission; marketing that elicits customer input to modify the mission; resource integration that tailors the goals of the mission; technology development that customizes the objectives of the goals; production that standardizes the products and services to meet the specifications of the objectives.

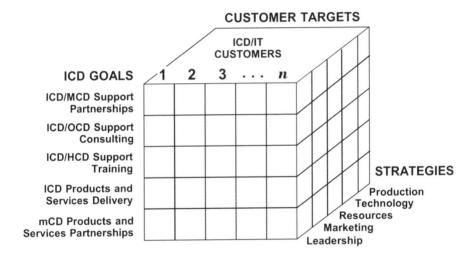

Figure 2-7. External Missioning Model

Phase 5—Internal Modeling

Finally, we positioned an internal organizational model for the implementation of the company's external mission (see Figure 2-8). Such a model is developed to service the goals, targets, and strategies of the external mission. The internal organizational functions are derived from our marketplace positioning, or MCD: policy, executive, management, supervision, delivery. The internal components of the organization include leadership, marketing, resources, technology, production. The internal processes of the organization are introduced in our strategies. In actuality, these processes are human processes: goaling, inputting, processing, planning, outputting.

As may be noted, this chapter has concerned the policy-level responsibilities of the internal organization. The primary responsibility of the internal policy level of the organization is marketplace positioning. As we will see in the next chapter, it remains for the executive level to "architect" the continuous alignment of the organization to fulfill this marketplace positioning.

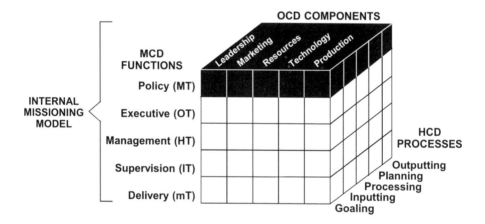

Figure 2-8. Internal Missioning Model

These five phases of marketplace positioning represent core processes for actualizing marketplace positioning as a source of wealth generation. Marketplace positioning by MCD has a profound impact upon the organization. It results in *external* communications with the marketplace to tell others who we are. It results in *internal* communications within our organization to orient everyone to what we must do to actualize our projected marketplace positioning.

MANAGING MCD

Here we will employ another real-life example of marketplace positioning. As indicated by Figure 2-9, this client company, too, possesses expertise in information technologies. To meet ICD requirements, the company has been developing software products in data and knowledge management. In addition, it has been developing management training and support programs focused primarily upon interpersonal skills (soft skills) and technical skills (hard skills).

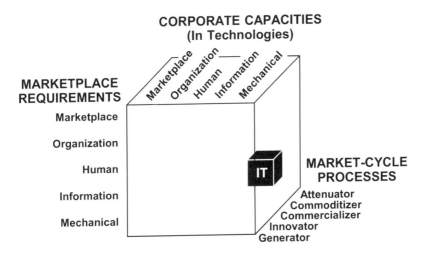

Figure 2-9. Current Image of IT Corporation

First of all, the company leaders began to process their primary target-level—ICD. This involved scaling the levels of ICD required by their customers. Table 2-6 illustrates these levels:

- **Data,** or data elements;

- **Information resources (IR),** or relationships between data elements;

- **Information resource development (IRD),** or multi-dimensional models of operations;

- **Information capital development (ICD),** or multidimensional models of phenomenal vectors;

- **Prime information capital development (ICD′),** or curvilinear multidimensional models of phenomena.

The leaders soon realized that their corporation met only the data and information-resource levels. They resolved to meet requirements for higher levels of ICD requirements for operational model building.

Table 2-6. Levels of ICD

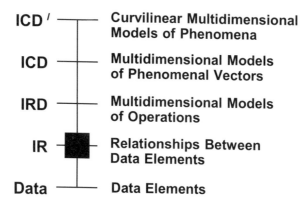

Secondly, the company leaders trained their sights on the levels of HCD requirements they were capable of addressing. We interpret the HCD levels, shown in Table 2-7, as follows:

- **Labor,** or physical skills (P);

- **Human resources (HR),** or physical and emotional skills (P • E);

- **Human resource development (HRD),** or physical, emotional, and intellectual skills (P • E • I);

- **Human capital development (HCD),** or physical, emotional, and individual intellectual processing skills (P • E^2 • I^3);

- **Prime human capital development (HCD′),** or prime physical, emotional, and interdependent intellectual processing skills (P • E^2 • I^5).

The leaders soon recognized that their current capacity addressed only the human resource (HR) level of HCD. They resolved to meet higher levels of HCD requirements for intellectual processing.

Table 2-7. Levels of HCD

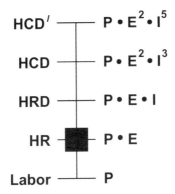

$$HCD' \longrightarrow P \bullet E^2 \bullet I^5$$

$$HCD \longrightarrow P \bullet E^2 \bullet I^3$$

$$HRD \longrightarrow P \bullet E \bullet I$$

$$HR \longrightarrow P \bullet E$$

$$Labor \longrightarrow P$$

Finally, the leaders envisioned a service and solutions arm to complement their software development (see Figure 2-10). To achieve this vision, they needed to develop an HCD capacity along with their ICD capacity. As may be noted, they required expertise in all of the complementary technologies in order to meet market-

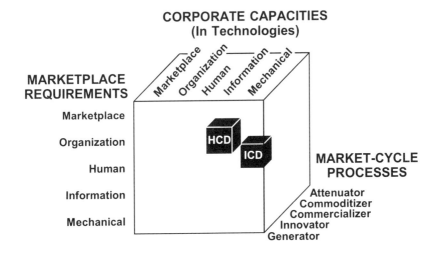

Figure 2-10. Visioning of Future IT Corporation

place requirements in ICD and HCD. In other words, they needed to transform their current operations as follows:

- IT into ICD in order to secure positioning in the commoditization market;

- HR into HCD in order to position in the commercialization market.

Together, these new capital developments would enable the software products to sell the consulting services, and the consulting services to sell the software products. Moreover, they would foster a synergistic relationship between the two dimensions to generate and innovate new products and services.

IN TRANSITION

The MCD model (Figure 2-11) supports continuous marketplace positioning. We position our corporate capabilities to meet marketplace requirements within the market life-cycle. In short, our positioning is our course and our *vision*. It will guide us to our future. Those organizations with good positioning know where they are headed. They are likely to grow. Those who lack perspective on their marketplace positioning may soon cease to exist!

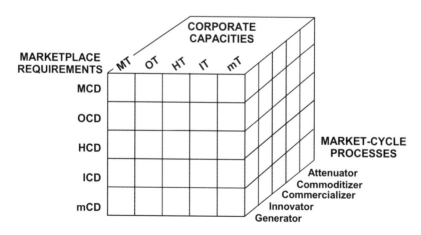

Figure 2-11. MCD Model

The marketplace itself is continuously evolving. Industry standards are coming into and going out of existence in brief periods of time; entire economies are coming into and going out of existence in similar periods. The twenty-first century promises a marketplace with all combinations of marketplace phenomena: birthing, growing, dying, transforming.

The global marketplace is an explosion of self-organizing phenomena. Generated by the tens of trillions of decisions made daily, the marketplace is, itself, a *"possibilities marketplace."* It is a continuously evolving marketplace to which we must respond intelligently.

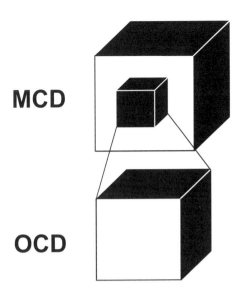

MCD

OCD

3 **Managing Organizational
Capital Development**

Organizational alignment fulfills marketplace positioning.

"The Team of Teams . . ."
—Modeling for Alignment

Positioned in the marketplace as an innovative standard-setter, Company B soon realized that they had a problem: their operations had reached a level of unmanageable complexity. To address this issue, they formed teams of exemplary engineers. Using the principles of concurrent engineering, they *"factored out"* all of the major operations of product building. They formed units representing major functions; then they factored within these major operations the primary functions upon which all unit components and processes had to bear.

In effect, the company formed a *"team of teams."* Here is the approach the team used. Their mission was to develop Total Product Modeling. Their goals were as follows:

1. To implement global concurrent engineering;

2. To implement collaborative organizational processes;

3. To change their engineering processes from serial to parallel and, ultimately, to rapid prototyping—concurrent processing.

Utilizing cross-functional analysis, the team of teams addressed the ingredients of their process-centric image (see Figure 3-1). Five major factors bore upon the process: co-orchestrated organizational change to keep up with changes in the marketplace; cooperative organizational teaming methods (such as their demonstration of process reengineering); collaborative human-processing methods; communicative information technologies; and coordinated mechanical tooling, including information connectivity.

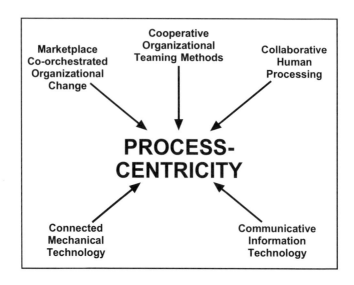

Figure 3-1. The Processing Ingredients

The team of teams believed they had an urgent need to technologize all of these areas in order to accomplish their mission of Total Product Modeling. We may view the focus of the team's technologizing effort in Table 3-1. As shown, their intent is to move upward from their current connectivity and communication to higher levels of objectives: collaboration, cooperation, co-orchestration. As also shown, each level of effort is defined by a level of new capital development: marketplace, organization, human, information, mechanical.

Table 3-1. Technologizing Objectives

5   Co-orchestration (Marketplace)
4   Cooperation (Organization)
3   Collaboration (Human)
2   Communication (Information)
1   Connectivity (Mechanical)

The vision of the basic model is represented below, in Figure 3-2. As may be noted, the functions are marketplace functions: organizational change to orchestrate alignment with continuous repositioning in the marketplace. In turn, the components are organizational teaming processes dedicated to cooperative work efforts such as the process reengineering. Finally, the processes are human processing systems dedicated to interdependent and collaborative processing. We may formulate this mission as the organizational capital development (OCD) mission:

Co-orchestrated organizational change functions are accomplished by organizational teaming components enabled by interdependent human processing.

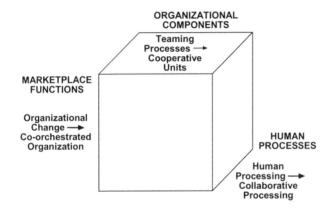

Figure 3-2. The Organizational Capital Development Mission

When we rotate our organizational teaming components deductively, or counterclockwise, they become the functions of our human capital development (HCD) mission (see Figure 3-3). In turn, the human processing systems become the components dedicated to accomplishing the teaming functions. Finally, new information processes are introduced. They accomplish the communication that enables the cooperative human-processing components to accomplish the collaborative organizational teaming functions. We may formulate this human capital mission as follows:

> *Cooperative organizational teaming functions are accomplished by collaborative human-processing components enabled by information-communication processes.*

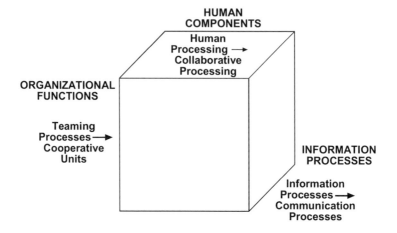

**Figure 3-3. The Human Capital
Development Mission**

By rotating our interdependent human-processing components deductively, they become the functions of our information capital mission (see Figure 3-4). In turn, information-communication processes become the components dedicated to accomplishing our human processing functions. Finally, new mechanical processes are introduced. They accomplish the connectivity that enables the information communication to accomplish the human processing functions. We may formulate this information capital mission in the following way:

> *Collaborative human-processing functions are accomplished by information-communication components enabled by mechanical connectivity.*

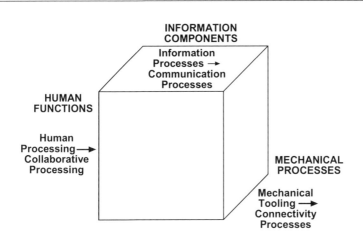

Figure 3-4. The Information Capital Development Mission

This is the basic paradigm for possibilities organization and organizational change. Change is a function of new capital development systems:

- MCD—Marketplace capital development,
- OCD—Organizational capital development,
- HCD—Human capital development,
- ICD—Information capital development,
- MCD—Mechanical capital development.

As we can see in Figure 3-5 (following page), each new capital development system is *nested* in the marketplace system: MCD, OCD, HCD, ICD, mCD. New capital development (NCD) is the source of all organizational change. It made a difference for the team of teams at Company B, and can make a difference for us and our organizations too.

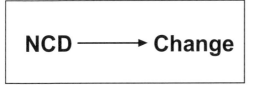

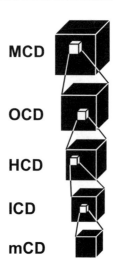

MCD

OCD

HCD

ICD

mCD

**Figure 3-5. The Possibilities Organization
as a Function of the New
Capital Development System**

If we compare Company B's approach to that of Company A
(see case study, Chapter 2), we find quite different results.
Whereas Company A's planning paradigm *"freezes"* product
design, Company B's processing paradigm *"frees"* products to
evolve in their most functional form. Thus, one company will
have a potentially infinite array of customized versions of a
standardized product-line; the other will have a potentially
infinite array of *"virtual"* on-the-shelf products that can be
tailored to specific customer requirements in the future.

Business possibilities begin with marketplace positioning, and
are actualized by aligning the organization with that positioning.
In this context, while marketplace positioning defines the future of
the corporation, nothing is possible if the organization is not
aligned to fulfill this positioning. Moreover, the reality of today's
business environment is the need for continuous realigning of
continuously repositioning organizations.

There are two basic kinds of alignment—**internal** and **external.**
Internal alignment is emphasized when we consider the internal operations of an organization, including its supplier partners and other extensions. In internal alignment, the organization is charged with the alignment of all of its resources and their transformation into new capital development systems: MCD, OCD, HCD, ICD, mCD. Basically, the organization contributes to NCD systems by aligning organizational resources with higher-order conditions:

- The organization is assembled (or "architected") and aligned to discharge marketplace positioning.

- Human processors are empowered and aligned to discharge the organization's architecture.

- Information is modeled and aligned to discharge human processes.

- Mechanical tooling is developed and aligned to discharge information models.

We can develop NCD systems internally in our organizations by:

- Continuously repositioning in the marketplace with MCD technologies;

- Continuously realigning the organization with OCD technologies;

- Continuously empowering human processing with HCD technologies;

- Continuously modeling information with ICD technologies;

- Continuously tooling mechanical instruments with mCD technologies.

External alignment is emphasized when we conceive of an organization in an interdependent relationship with other organizations. Increasingly, the science of organizational alignment is the science of business relationships between organizations. External alignment, then, emphasizes the interdependent relationships that must be developed and nourished in order to grow with continu-

73

ously changing marketplace requirements. In other words, we grow interdependently with the organizations with which our future is identified.

Our own organizational experience is relevant here. Not only have we developed NCD systems internally in our corporations using the practices explained above, but we have also established external relationships with other organizations. They provide us with three examples of external alignment:

1. At a simple level, our publishing firm is in partnership with another publishing firm. In this relationship, our press manages the marketing and fulfillment of the other's training products. This means that the organizations are aligned as follows: our management system is an extension of the other's executive system—they make and execute the policy; we manage its fulfillment.

2. Our consulting and training firm was conceived of in relationship with an office in the Federal sector. At the executive and management levels, we aligned our resources to fulfill their objectives: we related our executive-level functions to discharge their policy functions; we related our management-level functions to discharge their executive functions—and so on. In this manner, we helped to develop and implement the concept of indefinite quantity contracting in a Federal-sector profit center.

3. Finally, our R and D firm is in an interdependent and synergistic partnership with a major CAD-CAM firm. The mission is to develop the MCD, OCD, and HCD technologies that systematically interrelate organizational partners now focusing upon CAD-CAM contracts. In effect, we will do for organizations what is currently being done for design and manufacturing: computer-assisted innovation (CAI), computer-assisted organization (CAO), computer-assisted positioning (CAP). Thus we are designing the NCD software support system.

Business relationships are central to accomplishing organizational missions. Building and maintaining relationships through the alignment of organizations *is* the source of business. However, before we can relate externally to other organizations, we must understand the power and direction of our own organizations.

MODELING ORGANIZATIONAL ALIGNMENT

We may build a model of an organization by representing its functions, or intentions; its components, or delivery units; and its processes, or methods. The organization's functions are what it wants to accomplish. The organizations components are its resource capabilities. The organization's processes are its operational procedures.

We can employ this operational model for the purpose of organizational alignment. It will serve us in our responsibilities to align our organizations both internally and externally: internally within our own organizations and with our extended partners, and externally with other organizations and the marketplace. We label our model "OCD," or "organizational capital development." Building it involves four general steps:

1. Scaling the functions, or intentions, of the organization;

2. Scaling the components of the organization whose distributed capabilities and responsibilities will service the organization's functions;

3. Scaling the processes that the organizational components will apply to complete their responsibilities;

4. Representing the interaction of these elements of OCD in a three-dimensional way.

This chapter will provide a demonstration of how to carry out these steps.

We manage our organizational-alignment responsibilities by using our scaled OCD organizational information. We cross the organization's component capabilities with the organization's intentions to develop matrices of organizational information. By bringing these into interaction with the third scale, the processes of the organization, we develop a three-dimensional model of organizational information. These scales, matrices, and models provide us with useful material for aligning our organizations.

Our model building will help us answer critical organizational questions. Those questions include:

- *How do we build, or "architect," our organizations?*
- *How does our current organization operate?*
- *What are our organizations doing right?*
- *What are our organizations missing?*
- *Are our organizations aligned? Our resources? Our processes?*
- *Are we aligned with the conditions of the marketplace?*
- *Are our standards of performance aligned with the expectations and requirements of our customers?*

The growth and life of our organizations are dependent upon our answers to these questions.

Scaling Marketplace Functions

We begin by describing the functions, or intentions, of the organization (see Table 3-2). We derive the functions of our organization from our marketplace positioning. In other words, our organization is dedicated to functions derived from our marketplace positioning. The functional levels of any organization include:

- **Policy,** which uses marketplace technologies (MT) to define the organization's marketplace positioning;
- **Executive,** which uses organizational technologies (OT) to build, or "architect," the organization to align with the mission;
- **Management,** which uses human technologies (HT) to empower people and systems to perform within the organization's structure, or architecture;

- *Supervision,* often self-supervision today, which uses information technologies (IT) to manage information to service human performance;

- *Delivery,* which uses mechanical technologies (mT) to tool and retool to produce products and deliver services.

These functional levels are all dedicated to fulfilling marketplace positioning, which is derived from the marketplace conditions within which the organization exists.

Table 3-2. Scale of Organizational Functions

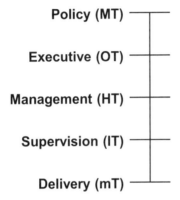

Policy (MT)

Executive (OT)

Management (HT)

Supervision (IT)

Delivery (mT)

This scale of organizational functions is an initial *map-in* to the goals of organizations. Deeper analyses of each level of these functions will provide a more detailed description of the specific organizational goals we expect our organization to accomplish. As we learn more about the performance requirements of each of these organizational levels, we will further define the goals of our organization.

Scaling Organizational Components

The next step in modeling is to define the organization's components (see Table 3-3). Our organizational processes were represented in the MCD external missioning and internal modeling: leadership, marketing, resources, technology, and production. The following terms are useful for redefining the organizational components of any organization:

- *Leadership* is responsible for developing new marketplace directions.

- *Marketing* is responsible for developing relationships with customers. This includes defining customer requirements.

- *Resource Integration* is responsible for developing solutions to fulfill customer needs.

- *Technology* is responsible for developing the designs needed to fulfill the resource-integration solutions.

- *Production* is responsible for producing products and delivering services.

Table 3-3. Organizational Components

This scale of organizational components is a helpful initial *map-in* for analyzing the distributed responsibilities of organizations. Further analyses of each of these unit capabilities will provide a clearer description of the capacities of the organizations that we need to build and align.

Organizational Capital Matrix

When we model an organization by aligning the organization's components to discharge its functions, we create the useful matrix shown in Table 3-4. As may be noted, the organizational components, or units, are aligned to discharge multiple levels of organizational functions, or intentions.

Table 3-4. The Organizational Capital Matrix

OCD COMPONENTS

MCD FUNCTIONS	Leadership	Marketing	Resources	Technology	Production
Policy					
Executive					
Management					
Supervision					
Delivery					

It is with this initial organizational matrix that we begin to see the distribution of our organization's units and intentions with clarity. This should stimulate many important questions about how our organizations are currently aligned and how they might be aligned. With this type of information, we may begin to build or rebuild our *organizational capital* as a source of wealth creation.

Scaling Human Processes

The last step in modeling an organization is to introduce the processes of the organization (see Table 3-5). These processes are described as human processes because people are the capital resources that drive the organization's processes. We scale them as follows:

- *Goaling,* or valuing measures;
- *Inputting,* or analyzing operations;
- *Processing,* or synthesizing operations;
- *Planning,* or operationalizing objectives;
- *Outputting,* or technologizing programs.

Table 3-5. Scale of Human Processes

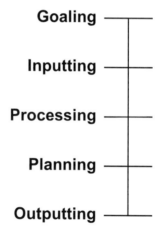

OCD Model

We complete our organizational model by adding the processes of the organization (see Figure 3-6). The objective of the OCD model may be succinctly expressed as thus:

> *The organization's positioning functions, or intentions, are discharged by leadership-driven organizational components, or units, enabled by goaling-driven organizational processes.*

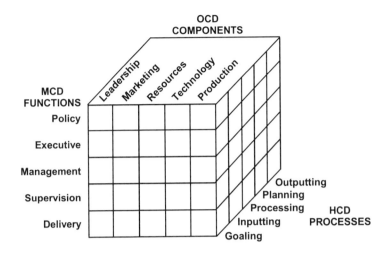

Figure 3-6. OCD Model

We begin organizational alignment by mapping our organizations with the OCD model. Once we have modeled our current operations, we will analyze how well our organization is aligned. Without an aligned organization, the performance of individuals may be for naught. Individuals will be oriented and then freed to maximize their contributions within the context of aligned organizations.

Next we will focus upon processes that enable us to model and manage the alignment of our organizations—to model and manage our *organizational capital.*

PROCESSES FOR ORGANIZATIONAL ALIGNMENT

We have defined the following processes for organizational alignment. These processes include five phases:

Phase 1: **Goal Alignment** for organizing and linking functions or goals;

Phase 2: **Resource Alignment** for organizing and linking component resources;

81

Phase 3:   **Process Alignment** for organizing and linking processes;

Phase 4:   **Customer Alignment** for aligning with the contexts or conditions of our business relationships;

Phase 5:   **Performance Alignment** for organizing and linking our measures of performance standards with customer organizations.

Through these processes we may model and manage our responsibilities to build and align our organizations.

Phase 1—Goal Alignment

The process of goal alignment involves organizing and linking the functions, or goals, of the organization. We organize goals by relating them. We begin by listing the intentions of the organization. These organizational intentions are collected within an existing organization or generated to create a new one. We then organize these goals by ordering them by the size or quality of their responsibilities:

- **Policy** is responsible for the organization's marketplace positioning or mission.

- The **executive** level is responsible for "architecting" the organization according to strategic organizational-level goals;

- The **management** level is responsible for systems-wide goals;

- **Supervision** handles system's objectives;

- **Delivery** is responsible for programmatic task performance and product development.

These levels are shown in Figure 3-7.

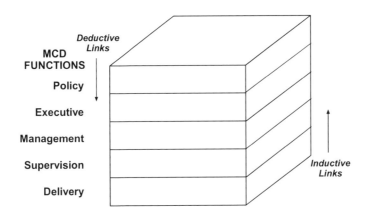

Figure 3-7. Goal Alignment

Finally, we align our goals by linking them. This involves communication links between and among those who are responsible for these various levels of organizational intentions. Once people in the organization are aware of the interrelational nature of these various levels of goals, they may align them with intentionality, deductively or inductively.

Aligned goals keep everyone in the organization honest. Everyone is expected to be able to articulate the goals for which they are responsible, as well as how those goals are related to higher-level goals and, ultimately, to the mission. Everyone must also be able to articulate how their goals impact upon lower-level systems, objectives, and performance goals that fulfill their goals. If the goals of an organization are not organized and linked, they are not aligned.

Phase 2—Resource Alignment

The process of resource alignment involves organizing and linking the organization's resources across organizational components, or units. We organize our resources by relating them. We begin by inventorying them. We may list them by name and description. We then relate our resources by ordering them. For example, we may organize them by their roles as components of an organization (see Figure 3-8). Here we see that the **leadership** component is composed of those resources necessary to develop marketplace positioning. The **marketing** component is resourced to fulfill leadership's positioning by relating to customers to collect customer requirements and to arrange product and service sales. **Resource integration** then takes the marketing handoff to integrate all resources to create solution designs. **Technology** resources then fill out the integrated design by bringing technological specialties to the solution plan. **Production** resources are required to fulfill the technological plans and deliver the organization's products and services.

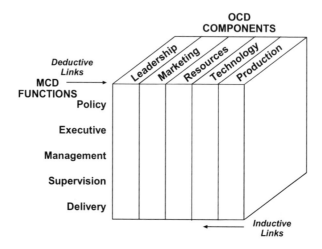

Figure 3-8. Resource Alignment

Finally, we align our resources by linking them. This involves communication links between and among those who are responsible for each of the organization's component units. Once people in the organization realize the interrelational nature of their component units, they may align them with intentionality.

Aligned resources keep everyone in the organization *mapped-in.* Everyone is expected to be able to articulate how information flows from their organizational units. Everyone must also be able to articulate how their outputs become inputs to other units. If the resources of an organization are not organized and linked, they are not aligned.

Phase 3—Process Alignment

The alignment of processes within an organization involves organizing and linking the processes. We organize our processes by relating them. We relate processes by ordering them. For example, we may relate our processes by ordering them according to their system's role: goaling and feedback processes, input processes, transformation processes, planning processes, and outputting processes (see Figure 3-9). Here we illustrate that all systems within an organization share common systems processes: every component and every functional level of an organization sets **goals,** collects **inputs,** designs **processes,** makes **plans,** and makes performance **outputs.** Process alignment means organizing processes in a way that maximizes the sharing of processing tools and processing time.

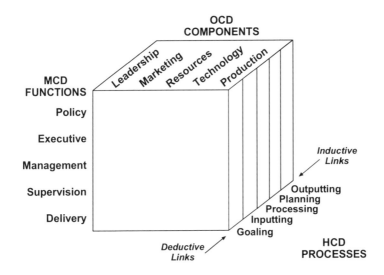

Figure 3-9. Process Alignment

Finally, we align our processes by linking them. This involves communication links between and among those who are responsible for these processes. Once people in the organization realize the interrelational nature of their processes, they may align them with intentionality.

Aligned processes keep everyone in the organization in motion. By linking information about processes, anyone can benefit from the process breakthroughs of anyone else. To accomplish this, everyone is expected to be able to articulate their operational processes. If the processes of an organization are not organized and linked, they are not aligned.

Phase 4—Customer Alignment

How well our organization aligns with the conditions of our customer organizations tells us whether we will remain in business. If we are poorly aligned with our customers, we can expect to go out of business, as they have no need for us. If we are tenuously aligned with our customers' businesses, our business relationships are also tenuous. If we are aligned and in *"sync"* with our customers, then we will have an opportunity to grow with them.

Aligning with customers means aligning our mutual organizations: functions, components, and processes. To align with our customers, we must understand their organizations. This involves organizing and linking our information about our customers and our own organization.

We organize customer information by relating to this information. We begin by inventorying what we know about our customers' goals (or functions), resources (or components), and processes. What are they trying to accomplish? What resources do they have? What are their current processes or methodologies? The results of our analyses will be information: operational specifications, systems drawings, and technologies that represent our customers.

We organize this information about customer functions, components, and processes by relating to them. We use our best understanding of any and all relevant technologies to help us in this organizing effort. For example, we may use our marketplace and organizational models to help us map our customers' marketplaces and our customer organizations (see Figure 3-10). By mapping customer information we will not only see what our customers are currently doing, but gain insight into what they are missing and what they could do in the future. This information is critical to building links with other organizations. These links are the functional links of all commerce.

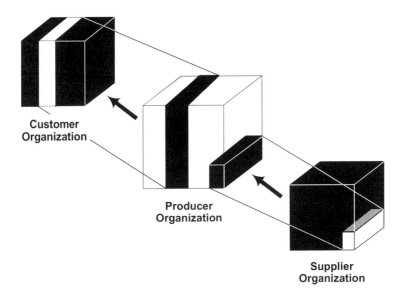

Figure 3-10. Customer Alignment

Finally, we link our organizations. Functionally, all organizations in the marketplace are linked. Part of one organization is an extension of another: *"I pay you for what you can do for me; you pay me for what I can do for you."* We are linked by these bonds of shared functions, components, and processes. Operationally, customer linking involves communication links between and among those who are responsible for their organizations. Once people realize the interrelational nature of their mutual organizations, they may align them with intentionality.

Aligned organizations define business. Our business is to keep our customers in business. If information about our customers' organizations is not organized and linked, then we are not aligned and we will soon be out of business.

Phase 5—Performance Alignment

How well our organization's performance aligns with our customers' standards tells us how well our business is likely to compete. If we perform up to expected standards, then we are in business. If we understand our customers so well that we can deliver performance beyond initial requirements, then we have contributed to making our customers more productive than their competitors. Now we have set new standards and are repositioned in the marketplace.

Aligning performance means providing our customers with what they need. To align our performance with our customers' needs, we must understand their current and future requirements. This involves organizing and linking our performance standards with the standards our customers expect and require.

We organize performance standards by relating to them. We begin by inventorying information about our customers' performance standards. Can we measure what our customers need? The results of our analyses will be lists of performance information that represent the performance measures our customers require. We use our best understanding of the performance measures of any and all relevant technologies to help us organize information about the performance measures of our customers (see Figure 3-11).

Finally, we link our organizations by exchanging performance information. Performance-information linking involves communication links between and among those who are responsible for measuring performance. Once people realize the interrelational nature of performance measures, they may align those measures with intentionality.

Aligned performance measures define interdependent business growth. If information about our customers' performance requirements is not organized and linked, there is no alignment, and our organization will be replaced by another organization whose performance measures are up to the changing performance requirements of the marketplace.

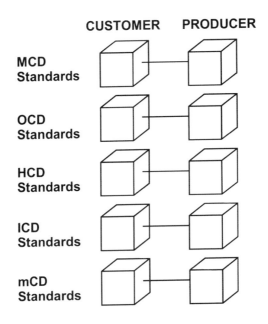

Figure 3-11. Performance Alignment

ALIGNING NEW CAPITAL DEVELOPMENT

New capital development has an impact upon every functional level, component unit, and process of the organization. All parts of the organization must relate to NCD:

- Marketplace positioning (MCD),
- Organizational alignment (OCD),
- Human processing (HCD),
- Information modeling (ICD),
- Mechanical tooling (mCD).

Everyone must relate to these NCD systems both *internally* within the organization and *externally* with the NCD systems of customers. How we define and relate these NCD systems tells us how they need to be aligned. Our understanding of NCD models impacts our decision-making regarding our alignment of goals, resources, processes, customers, and performance.

The mission of the organization is NCD: the development and alignment of all NCD systems. The following sections describe the alignment of organizational responsibilities for NCD.

Aligning MCD

Those responsible for aligning the organization to support marketplace positioning must focus their efforts upon MCD. The model of marketplace capital development below (Figure 3-12) identifies the MCD functions, components, and processes.

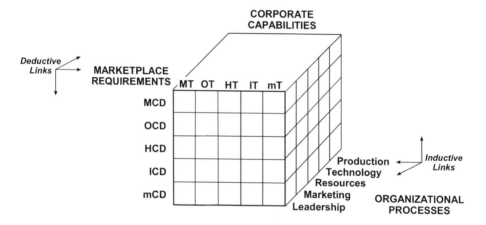

**Figure 3-12. Marketplace Capital
Development and Alignment**

Let us take a closer look at the dimensions of the model:

- The **functions** of MCD are derived from the market's requirements for NCD systems: MCD, OCD, HCD, ICD, and mCD. Essentially, the marketplace of organizations is dedicated to fulfilling these NCD requirements.

- As we saw in Chapter 2, the MCD **components** are the corporate technologies available among organizations in the marketplace: MT, OT, HT, IT, mT. These technologies are critical to meeting the requirements of the market-place.

90

- The **processes** of the MCD model are organizational processing systems: leadership, marketing, resources, technology, and production.

We can summarize these dimensions as follows:

Marketplace technologies are dedicated to new capital development enabled by organizational processing systems.

The relationships of these marketplace requirements, technological capabilities, and organizational processing systems define MCD. The interaction of these dimensions defines MCD alignment and the responsibilities of the **policy level** of the organization. Once we realize the interrelational nature of MCD, we may link these dimensions with intentionality, doing so deductively, inductively, or functionally.

Aligning OCD

Those responsible for aligning the organization to support organizational development and alignment must concentrate their efforts upon OCD (see Figure 3-13).

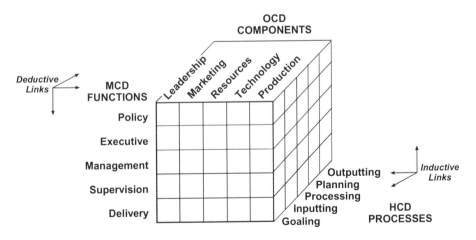

**Figure 3-13. Organizational Capital
Development and Alignment**

Again, let us take a closer look at our model's dimensions:

- The **functions** of OCD are derived from the market's technology requirements. These requirements are translated operationally into functional levels of the organization: policy (MT), executive (OT), management (HT), supervision (IT), and delivery (mT). In other words, the resources of the organization will be dedicated to fulfilling these marketplace requirements.

- The OCD **components** are units of the organizations, and are derived from the processes of the MCD model: leadership, marketing, resources (and their integration), technology, and production. These organizational units are critical to fulfilling market requirements.

- The **processes** of the OCD model are introduced as HCD processes: goaling, inputting, processing, planning, and outputting. These processes are essential for fulfilling the organization's goals.

We can succinctly express these dimensions as follows:

OCD components are dedicated to MCD functions enabled by HCD processing systems.

The relationship of MCD functions, OCD components, and HCD processes defines OCD. The interaction of these dimensions defines OCD alignment and the responsibilities of the **executive level** of the organization. Once we realize the interrelational nature of OCD, we may link its dimensions with intentionality, doing so deductively, inductively, or functionally.

Aligning HCD

Those responsible for aligning the organization to support the empowerment of human capital must focus upon HCD (see Figure 3-14).

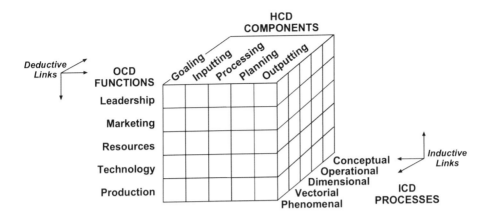

**Figure 3-14. Human Capital Development
and Alignment**

We may note the following about our model's dimensions:

- OCD components have become the HCD **functions:** leadership, marketing, resources (and their integration), technology, and production. Essentially, human capital is dedicated to fulfilling these organizational goals.

- Similarly, the HCD processes of the OCD model have become the HCD **components:** goaling, inputting, processing, planning, and outputting. These human processing components are critical to fulfilling the goals of the organization.

- Finally, the **processes** of the HCD model are introduced as ICD processes: phenomenal, vectorial, dimensional, operational, and conceptual. These ICD processes are essential for human processing; they are the processes through which the HCD components discharge OCD functions.

We may also note that each lower-order ingredient is dedicated to enabling the achievement of a higher-order purpose:

> *HCD components are dedicated to OCD functions enabled by ICD processes.*

These relationships of OCD functions, HCD components, and ICD processes define HCD. The interaction of these dimensions defines HCD alignment and the responsibilities of the **management level** of the organization. Once we realize the interrelational nature of HCD, we may link its dimensions with intentionality, doing so deductively, inductively, or functionally.

Aligning ICD

Those responsible for aligning the organization to support information capital development must concentrate their efforts upon ICD (see Figure 3-15).

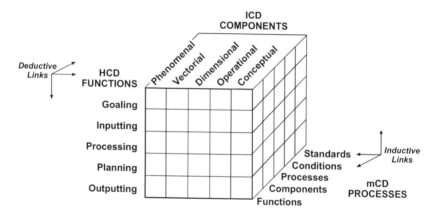

Figure 3-15. Information Capital Development and Alignment

We may note the following about our model's dimensions:

- The **functions** of ICD are derived from the HCD components: goaling, inputting, processing, planning, and outputting. Here, information capital is dedicated to service the requirements of thinking people.

- Likewise, the ICD **components** are derived from the ICD processes of the HCD model: phenomenal, vectorial, dimensional, operational, conceptual. These information components are critical ingredients in the service of human processing.

94

- Finally, the **processes** of the ICD model are introduced as mCD processes: functions, components, processes, conditions, and standards. These mCD operations enable the operationalizing processes and are essential to information capital processing.

Again, note that lower-order ingredients are dedicated to achieving higher-order purposes:

> *ICD components service HCD functions, or goals, through mCD processes.*

These interactions of HCD functions, ICD components, and mCD processes define ICD and its alignment and the responsibilities of the **supervisory level** of the organization. We may now link these dimensions with intentionality as well, deductively, inductively, or functionally.

Aligning mCD

Those responsible for aligning the organization to support mechanical capital development must focus their efforts upon mCD (see Figure 3-16).

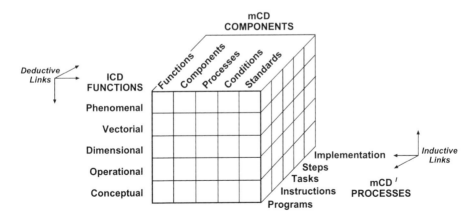

Figure 3-16. Mechanical Capital Development and Alignment

As we can see, the following describes our model's dimensions:

- The ICD components have become the **functions** of mCD: phenomenal, vectorial, dimensional, operational, and conceptual. Mechanical components, or tools, are dedicated to service information designs, or ICD.

- In turn, the mCD processes of the ICD model have become mCD **components:** functions, components, processes, conditions, and standards. These mechanical components are critical to fulfilling information designs.

- Finally, new mCD′ programming **processes** are introduced: programs, instructions, tasks, steps, and implementation. These programmatic mechanical processes are essential to mechanical processing.

Once again, lower-order ingredients are dedicated to higher-order purposes:

> *The mCD components service ICD functions through mCD′ processes.*

The interaction of these dimensions and their relationships define mCD and its alignment and the responsibilities of the **delivery level** of the organization. We may now also link these dimensions with intentionality, doing so deductively, inductively, or functionally.

ALIGNING DELIVERY SYSTEMS

Aligning Internal Delivery Systems

Just as the dimensions of capital development systems may be related by the external rotations of model building, so may organizational dimensions be related and rotated *internally* within the organization. The illustrations in Figure 3-17 are straight deductive rotations of the driving components and functions of the internal delivery systems of organizations. We can see that in the organization's delivery systems, the leadership component drives the policymaking functions; marketing drives the executive-level functions; resource integration drives the management-level functions; technology development drives the supervisory-level functions; and production drives the delivery-level functions.

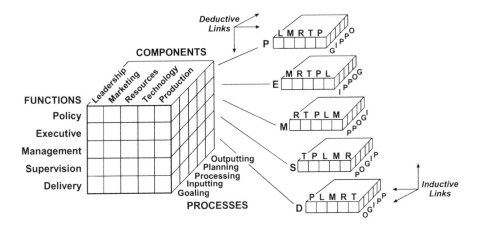

Figure 3-17. Internal Alignment of Delivery Systems

If we follow the vector of any one of the organizational functions, we may discriminate the primary responsibilities of the unit. For example, at the policy level, we find goal-driven components dedicated to accomplishing leadership-driven functions. In a similar manner, we may discern the responsibilities of the executive level: customer-inputting-driven components dedicated to marketing-driven functions. Likewise, we may discriminate the responsibilities of the management level: generative-processing-driven components dedicated to resource-integration-driven functions. Also, we may find the responsibilities of the supervisory or teaming level: planning-driven components dedicated to technology-driven functions. Finally, we may discover the primary responsibilities of the delivery level: outputting-driven components dedicated to production-driven functions. These discriminations are illustrated in Table 3-6.

Table 3-6. Primary Responsibilities of Functional Levels

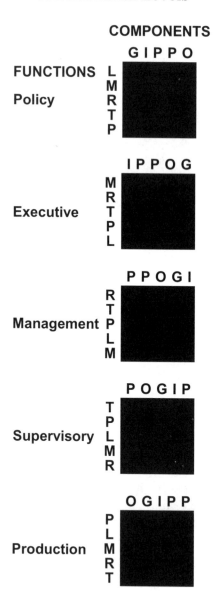

COMPONENTS

G I P P O

FUNCTIONS L
M
Policy   R
T
P

I P P O G

M
R
Executive T
P
L

P P O G I

R
T
Management P
L
M

P O G I P

T
P
Supervisory L
M
R

O G I P P

P
L
Production M
R
T

Aligning External Delivery Systems

In turn, *external* alignment between organizations may follow the same paradigm as internal alignments within organizations. When relating interdependently to other organizations, for example, we may relate as illustrated in Figure 3-18. Notice that the organizations are interdependently related by aligning their functional levels of operations externally:

- Producer policy with customer policy;
- Executive architecture with executive architecture;
- Management systems with management systems;
- Supervisory objectives with supervisory objectives;
- Producer delivery tasks with customer tasks.

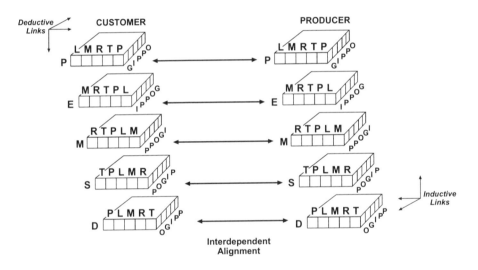

Figure 3-18. Interdependent External Alignment of Delivery Systems

This *interdependent alignment* means the organizations are committed to interdependent processing: mutual processing for mutual benefit.

We may also relate dependently, as when serving a customer organization (see Figure 3-19). In viewing our illustration, we may note the following:

99

- Policymaking is conducted by the customer organization without assistance from the producer organization.

- The servicing organization aligns its policy functions with the executive architectural functions of the customer organization.

- The other operations are aligned by continuing to rotate and relate the functions, components, and processes of both organizations.

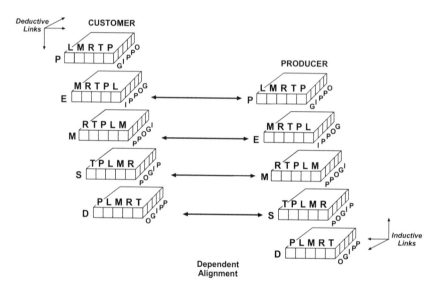

Figure 3-19. Dependent External Alignment of Delivery Systems

This *dependent alignment* means that the producer organization is in a dependent relationship with the customer organization, serving a level below its capabilities.

Again, the primary responsibilities of the different functional levels may be determined in precisely the same way as those shown in Table 3-6. First, discriminate the organization function vectors. Second, rotate the organizational components deductively to become functions. Third, rotate the organizational processes deductively to become components. We dedicate these components to discharging these elaborated functions.

In the Carkhuff Group, we believe that the organization is the implementing vehicle of marketplace positioning. We believe in the future of the *"possibilities organization"*—an organization that continuously realigns its corporate resources to implement continuous repositioning in the marketplace. This belief means that we need a model that is flexible and changeable, yet systematic: one that can guide as well as track the alignment of an organization's functions, components, and processes. This is why we developed the OCD model.

In this context, we can see organizational alignment in operation in the *external alignment* of the new divisions (Figure 3-20). As shown below, the executive level of the OCD division is aligned with the executive level of MCD division. Similarly, the management level of HCD division is aligned with the management level of OCD division. And so on! This alignment means that the capital development systems of the Carkhuff Group flow deductively from higher-order to lower-order systems: MCD, OCD, HCD, ICD, mCD.

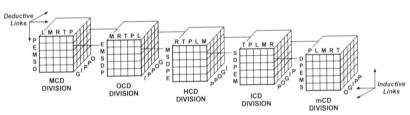

Figure 3-20. External Alignment of Divisions

We can also view OCD in operation in the *internal alignment* of the new MCD division (Figure 3-21). In a deductive flow, policy is leadership-driven; the executive level is market-driven; the management level is resource-driven; the supervisory level is technology-driven; and the delivery level is production-driven. This means that the drivers of delivery systems of the MCD division flow deductively from higher-order to lower-order systems: leadership, marketing, resource integration, technology, production.

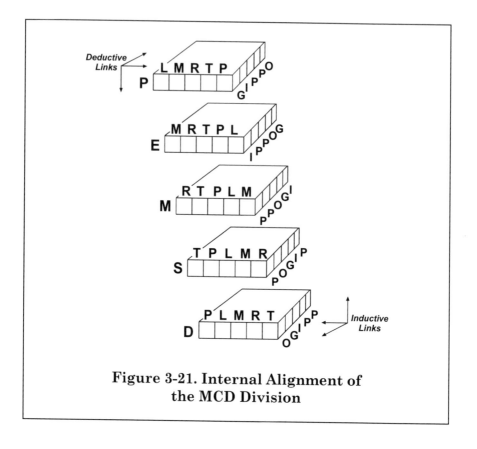

Figure 3-21. Internal Alignment of the MCD Division

IN TRANSITION

The OCD model (Figure 3-22) supports continuous organizational alignment with continuously changing marketplace positioning. This model is essential, for although we may align our organizations internally and externally in a number of other ways, there remains three important issues:

- *Are our organizational alignments operational?*

- *Are their functions, components, and processes appropriate?*

- *Are their conditions and standards known?*

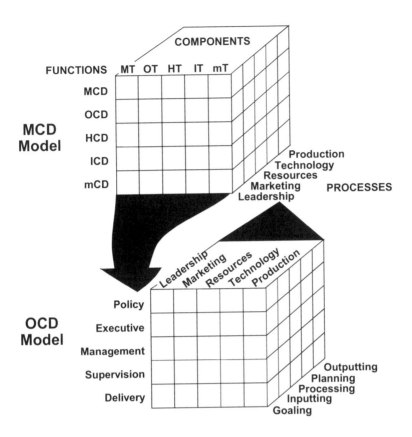

Figure 3-22. MCD–OCD Models

In the final analysis, the continuously aligning organization is a *"possibilities organization"* capable of instantaneously aligning resources to serve continuously changing marketplace requirements. In short, possibilities organizations enable us to engage in continuous processing to generate our own destinies with intelligence and intentionality. An aligned organization supports the acceleration of evolution: we no longer have to endure the painfully slow, incidentally random, and often destructive processes of an organization that is anything less than a *"possibilities organization."*

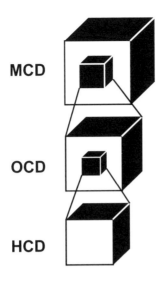

MCD

OCD

HCD

4 Managing Human Capital Development

> *Human processing is the source of all generation and innovation.*

"The Monolithic Idea"
—A Model of Human Processing

It was July 1958. Jack Kilby was alone in the lab because everyone else was on vacation. He had an idea of incalculable significance. He only hoped his boss would let him try the idea once or twice to see if it would work.

Kilby's idea was to integrate all the parts of an electronic circuit. He was successful in his efforts, eventually integrating the resistors, transistors, capacitors, and diodes in a single monolithic block of semi-conductor material.

The principle was labeled "The Monolithic Idea" in honor of the monolithic integrated circuit. Today, the invention is better known as the semi-conductor chip. The implications of this technological innovation were—and still are—profound. Already, less than half a century later, the chip has pervaded our land, sea, and sky. It functions at the heart of our deep-space probes and our space shuttles. It is the core of our deep-sea sensors. On Earth, it drives our clocks, cameras, toasters, word processors, and perhaps most critically, our communications networks. Spurred on by the convergence of micro-electronics and digital technologies, the computer and telecommunications industries have been able to take a giant step toward achieving an unimpeded flow of global information.

The semi-conductor chip has made possible astonishing reductions in the size, cost, and power requirements of electronic equipment. As a technological innovation, the chip is smaller, lighter, faster, cheaper to make, and more reliable than traditional circuits. Indeed, the chip's raw material, silicon, is derived from ordinary sand, one of Earth's most plentiful elements. Finally, while the manufacture of microchips can be demanding, it does not pollute Earth's land, sea, and sky.

The chip's most important implications may be human rather than simply technological. The chip has made computers almost universally available. A single chip, driven by inexpensive batteries, is faster, more reliable, and more powerful than the largest, most energy-consuming computer of the 1950s. In a very real sense, the microchip brought about the end of the Industrial Age and ushered in the Electronics, or Data, Revolution. As simple machinery once enhanced humankind's physical power and freed people from the back-breaking drudgery of physical labor, now the tiny silicon chip enhanced humankind's intellectual power and freed people from the drudgery of mind-numbing intellectual labor. Like all true revolutions, it introduced the prospect of a new age: the Information Age.

What makes Kilby's contributions profound is not the products they generate, but the generative processes they employ. In other words, Kilby has a thinking system—a processing system—for generating *"breakthroughs."* Here is how he initiates and engages in that system.

In an interview with Dr. David N. Aspy, an associate of ours, Kilby spelled out his entry step in processing. Essentially, he immerses himself in the subject matter or substance of any phenomenon on which he is working. This period of immersion can take weeks or even months. During this time, he conquers the operations involved and develops preliminary models to reflect the operations.

After this period of time, he begins to process individually to generate his first new images of the phenomenon. What does he do with his new image of the phenomenon? He censors it! As Kilby says, *"Any idea discovered so readily cannot be all that powerful."*

Moreover, he shares the phenomenal image with his colleagues. He stimulates them to generate and share their images. Most important, they treat all images as input to interpersonal processing of new and more powerful images.

Finally, Kilby lives and processes inside the phenomenal images he and his colleagues have generated. He dedicates himself along with other phenomenal components to accomplishing the phenomenal functions. He employs the phenomenal processes to enable the components to accomplish the function. In effect, he merges with the phenomena. What he has generated, he now innovates.

Kilby is an exemplar for all generative processing. He builds models of the phenomenal operations. He processes these operations generatively—individually, interpersonally, and finally, interdependently.

Processing is all about phenomena. Phenomena are the people, data, and things that we encounter in our daily existence. They may be as small as a skill step in a task we must perform. They may be as large as the great mission of our business, our economy, or our society. Every experience is phenomenal.

Phenomena are defined by their operations: the functions they discharge; the components they invest; the processes in which they engage; the conditions from which they derive; the standards they set. In essence, phenomena are processing systems: component inputs are transformed into function outputs by processes under specifiable conditions and with measurable standards.

Human processing, then, is about generating phenomena: qualitatively improved images of phenomenal functions, components, processes, conditions, and standards. Ultimately, we learn to live and process within the phenomena we have generated. We label this "innovative processing" as we seek to improve the implementation of the phenomenal dimensions.

Human processing is what human capital development, or HCD, is all about. Human processing for generating qualitatively better and more powerful images of the phenomena with which we work! Human processing for innovating qualitatively better and more powerful dimensions within the phenomena with which we work!

To be sure, Kilby became the model for human processing in the twentieth century. Yet each and every one of us may become generative processing models in the twenty-first century. It is the only way to keep abreast of the spiraling changes of our time. It is the only way to make our contributions to these changes.

The history of human capital and the history of economic need are partners.

When business and industry needed labor in the Industrial Age, they looked for people to serve as extensions of machinery. If people could perform the physically conditioned responses that were required, they had the job. Some would be hired to set goals and make plans; but most people were expected to do the output work that could not be mechanized. In short, the human-capital requirement of the Industrial Age was physical performance.

With the Data Age in the second half of the twentieth century came a change in business and industry requirements for the labor pool. Micro-electronic-driven machinery reduced the number of agricultural and manufacturing jobs. These same micro-electronic technologies enabled a tremendous growth in service businesses. The implications were profound. More of the labor pool was hired as managers and supervisors to process information. Everyone else had to be able to make plans, lots of plans, and then fulfill the outputs of these plans. Soon, computers made the term "optional features" ubiquitous. Product catalogs began growing by measures of magnitude. As a result of all the above, the average worker needed knowledge and skills beyond the conditioned physical-performance requirements of the Industrial Age.

Today, most people must have some level of technical skill in order to work their way through the veritable maze of information. Although not everyone may be developing work plans or steps from scratch, the number of unique options makes every task, for all purposes, a "new plan." For managers and supervisors, the situation has meant not only acquiring technical skills, but also developing what has come to be known as human skills or "soft skills." When we analyze management "soft skills" for their core ingredient, they factor to "interpersonal communication skills." Requirements for interpersonal communication skills have now filtered down to nearly every worker, usually in some form of training in customer-service skills. In short, the Data Age has changed human-resource requirements from physical performance to technical knowledge and interpersonal communications.

The old order is continuing to unravel. More and more people are becoming entrepreneurs and intrapreneurs. More and more people are now required to take responsibility for their own performance, from start to finish. Many are expected to perform tasks that were once the sole domain of an elite class of business leaders and management: to set goals and direction, collect and analyze information inputs, process or make decisions about this information, and conquer planning technologies as well as perform output tasks. Furthermore, the skills in each of these areas of goaling, analyzing, processing, planning, and outputting are growing in depth and sophistication. In short, the twenty-first century is changing the requirements for human capital. With physical performance now minimized by automation, technical knowledge and interpersonal communications are simply base-line skills. No one can do without them, but they are not enough. The growing requirement for human capital is *"intellectual skills."* Everyone needs to be able to process—to think! But what does this really mean? What are these *"intellectual skills"*?

This chapter is about human capital development and how we can model and measure its dimensions. It is also about empowering people in the intellectual skills that are becoming the new requirements for the twenty-first century and beyond.

MODELING HUMAN PROCESSING

We may build a model of human capital by representing people's functions, or intentions; their components, or parts; and related transformation processes, or how people service these functions. The functions of people are defined by what they intend to accomplish. The components of people are defined by their ingredients and how those ingredients are related. The processes of human processing are defined as the methods that can be applied to generate change in the service of human intentions.

With the information above, we can construct an operational model that will serve us in our responsibilities to develop and manage people. We label our model "HCD," or "human capital development." Building it involves four general steps:

1. Scaling the functions, or intentions, of people.

2. Scaling the human-skills components, or ingredients, that will service these functions;

3. Scaling the transformation processes that can be applied to introduce change, and so to complete their responsibilities;

4. Representing the interaction of these elements of HCD in a three-dimensional way.

A demonstration of these steps will be presented in the following pages.

Once we understand how to model HCD, we will be able to manage our responsibilities for human processing by using our HCD model. We will begin by asking ourselves to scale what we know about human performance. We then will cross information about human components with information about the functions of people to develop matrices of information about human capital development. By bringing these into interaction with a third scale, a scale of transformation processes, we will develop three-dimensional models of information about human capital. Scaling, matrixing, and modeling thus provide us with highly useful methods for developing and managing information about people.

Our model building will help us answer critical questions about human capital development and performance management. Those questions include:

- *How do we generate and represent information about people and their performance?*

- *What are our current methods and policies regarding the modeling of human skills and human performance?*

- *What current practices are effective?*

- *What critical practices are missing?*

- *Is our information about people modeled and currently available?*

- *Are our various forms of human performance related to information?*

- *Are our standards of performance in human capital development and performance management aligned with the expectations and requirements of our customers?*

The development of our people and our organizations depends upon our answers to these questions.

Scaling Organizational Functions

Within the business context, the functions of people are to service organizational goals. Another way to say this is that the intentions of people are to serve the requirements generated by organizational alignment. To describe the functions of people, we look to our model of organizational capital development (OCD). We derive information about human responsibilities from the components of our OCD model, as illustrated in Table 4-1.

Table 4-1. Organizational Functions

Leadership	Managing new directions
Marketing	Managing market relationships
Resources	Managing tailored solutions
Technology	Managing customized services
Production	Managing standardized products

This scale of responsibilities gives us an initial *"map-in"* to orient us to the intentions of people. Further analyses of each level of these functions will provide a deeper understanding and a more clearly defined description of the specific intentions that organizations have for their employees and associates. As we learn more about each of these levels of distributed requirements, we will further define the functions of people.

By defining these functions, we begin to see the imbedded requirements that come from the organization and its positioning in the marketplace. Do our people serve the process of organizational alignment and organizational performance? If not, then our people are not contributing to the growth of the organization. The next step in our model building will help us address any uncertainties about whether our people are contributing to the growth of the organization.

Scaling Human Components

In this step of modeling HCD, we define human components, or ingredients. (Later sections in this chapter will further elucidate what we mean by these components.) The human components are scaled as shown in Table 4-2. In viewing the scale, we may recall that the human components were introduced as processes in our OCD model. They include the skills that people need in order to do the following:

- Set **goals,**
- Analyze **input** about current operations,
- **Process,** or synthesize, new operations,
- **Plan,** or operationally define, the steps needed to fulfill new operations,
- **Output,** or perform, new programs.

116

Table 4-2. Human Components

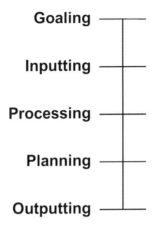

Goaling

Inputting

Processing

Planning

Outputting

This scale of human components is a useful initial *map-in* for analyzing the quality of our human capital resources. Further analyses of this information will provide us with a more detailed description of the kinds of human performance skills we need to develop.

By defining human performance skills, we have tools for analyzing the quality of human performance. Do our people best serve the intentions of the organization? If not, then we should consider transforming them into more useful components. These components of human performance are also the processes of organizational performance: goaling, inputting, processing, planning, and outputting.

Human Capital Matrix

We begin to see the value of modeling human capital when we represent performance-skills components, or ingredients, in relation to the functions of the organization. We do this by creating what we call the Human Capital Matrix (see Table 4-3). The matrix presents us with a visual model of how human components are aligned to discharge multiple levels of organizational intentions. In other words, it shows us that the HCD components are dedicated to discharging functions of the organization.

Table 4-3. Human Capital Matrix

HCD COMPONENTS

OCD FUNCTIONS	Goaling	Inputting	Processing	Planning	Outputting
Leadership					
Marketing					
Resources					
Technology					
Production					

Equipped with the Human Capital Matrix, we begin to see the distribution of our information about our people and their responsibilities. The matrix should stimulate many important questions about the quality and availability of the human capital that we have or need in order to service the processes of our organizations. With this window on human performance requirements, we may start to build our *human capital.*

Scaling Information Processes

The next step in building our HCD model is to introduce the information processes that enable the human components to discharge their organizational functions. (Later, in Chapter 5, we will take a closer look at these processes.) As we can see in Table 4-4, they include processes for the following:

- **Conceptual modeling,** or conceptual information and data;

- **Operational modeling,** or operational information;

- **Dimensional modeling,** or multidimensional information;
- **Vectorial modeling,** or the forces or conditions of phenomena;
- **Phenomenal modeling,** or the phenomena themselves.

These processes of information transformation provide the final piece of our model of HCD.

Table 4-4. Information Processes

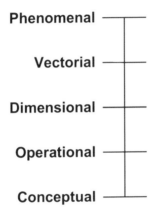

HCD Model

We complete our HCD model by adding the processes of information transformation (see Figure 4-1). The objective of the HCD model may be succinctly expressed in this way:

> *The functions, or intentions, of the organizations*
> *are discharged by skilled human components*
> *enabled by information processes.*

In other words, the ICD processes enable the HCD components to discharge OCD functions.

We begin the analysis and development of our human capital by scaling, matrixing, and modeling our human-capital information using the HCD model. Once we have modeled this current

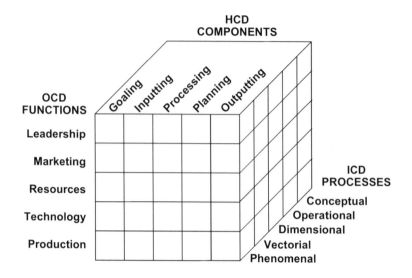

Figure 4-1. HCD Model

information about our human capital, we will see its implications for recruitment, selection, promotion, placement, training and development, performance management, and even compensation. Without a comprehensive understanding of information about our human capital, we will be missing huge opportunities for utilizing the human capital needed to grow our organizations. With an understanding of this information, we may elevate the performance of our people to maximize their contributions within the context of our aligned, marketplace-positioned organizations.

Next, we will focus upon better understanding the processes of human performance. This will help us improve our processes for modeling and managing our *human capital,* and for developing them as powerful sources of wealth.

PROCESSES FOR HUMAN PROCESSING

Managers have long been discharging the operations of the organization:

- **Goaling** by measuring the assigned tasks, including their attendant values and requirements;

- **Inputting** by receiving relevant and inclusive databases;
- **Processing** by thinking to generate solution designs;
- **Planning** by detailing the steps to accomplish the designs;
- **Outputting** by implementing the steps to accomplish the designs.

Our human capital may have been competent in their responsibilities to goal, input, plan, and output. What they have not done *well* or have not done *at all* is process. Either they do not process systematically or they do not process at all!

What we will introduce here are systematic processes for human processing. We call these core human processes I^5 **skills.** The I^5 skills define systematic processes for human processing:

- I^1—Information relating to define phenomenal operations;
- I^2—Information representing to dimensionalize images of phenomena;
- I^3—Individual processing to generate new images of phenomena;
- I^4—Interpersonal processing to generate more powerful images of phenomena;
- I^5—Interdependent processing to generate the most powerful images of phenomena.

These skills are shown in Figure 4-2. Note that while the I^5 processing systems are emphasized in the processing phase of HCD processing, they apply to all phases of processing: goaling, inputting, planning, and outputting, as well as processing. This

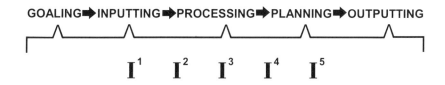

GOALING➡INPUTTING➡PROCESSING➡PLANNING➡OUTPUTTING

$$I^1 \quad I^2 \quad I^3 \quad I^4 \quad I^5$$

Figure 4-2. HCD Processing Phases

121

means that we now have a system for processing generatively to enable organizational components and discharge marketplace functions.

- The key to *"doing the right thing"* is found in the early phases of goaling and inputting, and culminates in processing.

- The key to *"doing things right"* is found in the follow-on phases of planning and outputting.

In short, the I^5 processing implements all phases of HCD processing and accounts for all processing (see Figure 4-3). Here we will approach the I^5 skills developmentally; keep in mind that the skills are, themselves, interdependent systems that can be entered at any stage and instantaneously related to all stages. Now let us take a look at these core I^5 skills for human processing.

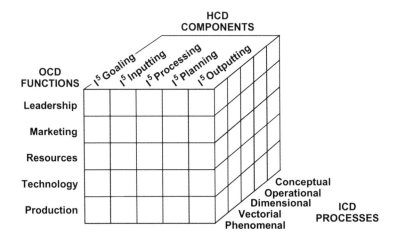

Figure 4-3. "I^5" *Nested* in the HCD Model

I^1—Information Relating Systems

Processing is first and foremost an information science. We relate to our concepts of human experience in order to transform them into operations that we can act upon. In other words, we seek to *operationalize* them.

In the absence of conceptual information, we relate to the phenomena themselves. We do so in order to elicit information, albeit conceptual information. Interrelating systems are preconditions for information relating.

Information relating systems generate operational information. Most information is not operational. Most information is conceptual.

One system for representing information is composed of data, information, knowledge, wisdom, and creativity. Beyond data, none of the definitions themselves are operational; information is defined by relating two or more data elements; knowledge is not even defined at the level of principles. To sum, all levels of definition are represented at low levels of conceptual information.

The levels of conceptual information to be transformed are shown in Table 4-5. These levels are defined verbally as follows:

- **Facts** are the labels that we attach to things.

- **Concepts** are the relationships between things.

- **Principles** are the explanations for the relationships.

- **Applications** are the contexts for the relationships.

- **Objectives** are the operations for the relationships.

Table 4-5. Levels of Conceptual Information

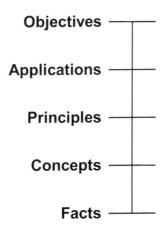

Objectives

Applications

Principles

Concepts

Facts

In turn, the levels of operational information are illustrated in Table 4-6. We define these operational levels as follows:

• **Functions** are outputs such as products and services.

• **Components** are inputs such as parts or participants.

• **Processes** are procedures that transform components into processes.

• **Conditions** are the contexts or environments for this processing.

• **Standards** are the level of excellence or achievement for this processing.

Table 4-6. Levels of Operational Information

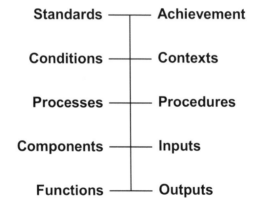

The operations of the levels of conceptual information are scaled in Table 4-7. Note that conceptual information culminates in objectives that are fully operational processing systems:

Component inputs are transformed into function outputs by processes under specifiable conditions and with measurable standards.

Table 4-7. Information Relating Systems
(Operations of Conceptual Information)

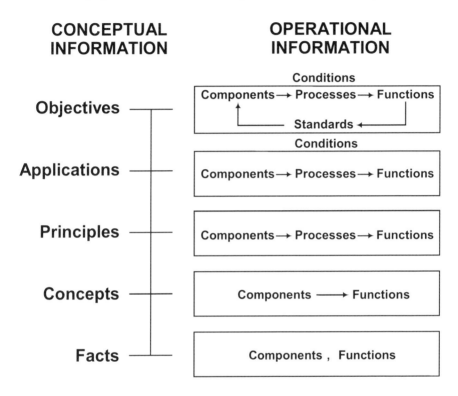

Information relating systems enable information representing systems: together, these systems constitute the preparation for processing. They serve to introduce managers and phenomena to phenomenal possibilities.

Our first step in human processing, then, is relating to information (see Figure 4-4). As may be noted, I[1] systems enable us to transform stimulus (S) material or experience into operational responses (R). We thus transform the conceptual information by operationalizing it: functions (F), components (C), processes (P), conditions (C), standards (S)—or FCPCS.

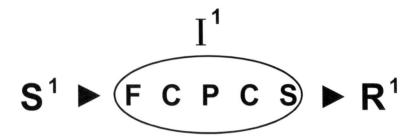

Figure 4-4. Information Relating Systems

The I^1 systems are preconditions for all processing: if we cannot define operational information, then we cannot process generatively.

I^2—Information Representing Systems

Processing is, secondly, a modeling science. Information representing transforms operational information into multidimensional models.

Information representing is the next stage in processing. The goal of information representing is to produce dimensional images of phenomena. In other words, we transform operational images into dimensional images. The dimensional images are represented by three-dimensional models of operations: functions, components, processes, conditions, and standards. All of this is accomplished with our skills in information representing, or I^2. We represent phenomena as a precondition for processing with them. We cannot process what we have not represented.

In representing information at the highest levels, then, we represent the dimensionality of phenomenon in some meaningful way. Although there are many levels of information representing systems, *dimensionalized information* is the most powerful and useful information representing system. Dimensional information includes:

- **1D,** or one-dimensional, linear information;

- **2D,** or two-dimensional, matrixed information;

- **3D,** or three-dimensional modeled information;

- **ND,** or *nested,* three-dimensional modeled information;

- **MD,** or multidimensional modeled information.

We may view the systems of dimensional information representing in the scale below (Table 4-8). This skills outline is presented developmentally, from 1D, 2D, 3D to *nested* (ND) and multidimensional (MD) information representation. Cumulatively, these skills enable us to represent dimensional images of any phenomena.

Table 4-8. Information Representing Systems

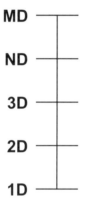

Information representing systems enable us to transform phenomenal operations into multidimensional models. As shown in Figure 4-5, the phenomena are defined by their functions, components, and processes. In turn, the latter are derived from the superordinate phenomenal conditions in which they exist. These phenomenal conditions have their own operations: functions, components, processes. Finally, the phenomena generate their own phenomenal standards of performance, which are defined by their own operations.

CONDITIONS

PHENOMENA

STANDARDS

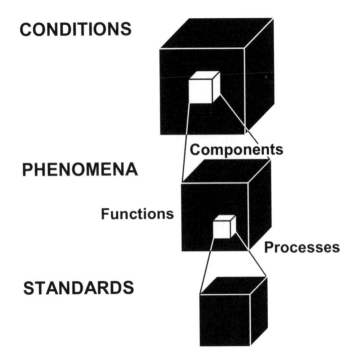

Components

Functions

Processes

Figure 4-5. Information Representing Incorporates Information Operations

While information representing is a skill, it is also an attitude: an attitude of respect, an attitude of commitment, an attitude of perseverance. Respect for the complexity of phenomena! Commitment to actualizing its potential! Multidimensional information modeling communicates this respect. That is because *multidimensional* emphasizes *interdependency*. It is the interdependent processing of multidimensional systems that yields growth for all parties. Accurate information representing is a critical requirement for the possibilities manager in the twenty-first-century global marketplace.

Operational information is linear. Dimensional information is multidimensional: it represents all levels of dimensions in their various interactions (see Figure 4-6). Dimensional information is thus essential as well for the twenty-first-century possibilities manager.

128

I² skills represent the phenomena by dimensionalizing their images: 1D, 2D, 3D, *nested*-D, multi-D. We can see how the I² systems transform the phenomenal images from R¹ to R².

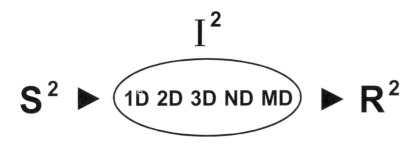

Figure 4-6. Information Representing Systems

The I² systems provide the necessary building blocks for processing—dimensional images of the phenomena to be processed. Dimensional information represents our understanding of the complexity and power of phenomena. Information representing prepares us for individual processing, or thinking: the skills to process the information that we have represented.

I³—Individual Processing Skills

Processing, thirdly, is a generative processing science. *Processing* means transforming stimulus inputs into response outputs. *Generative processing* means transforming stimulus inputs into response outputs that the stimuli were not intended to elicit! In other words, the processor generates *new responses*. In so doing, the processor also generates a *new stimulus environment!*

Individual processing is *possibilities thinking*. Possibilities thinkers begin by goaling systematically. The operative word here is *"systematically."* They analyze current operations: Did they achieve their goals? If not, they synthesize images of more productive operations, expanding alternatives and then narrowing to preferred courses. This is where information representing contributes. Our ability to expand and narrow operations within synthesizing is contingent upon the quality of our model-building activity. Next, possibilities thinkers rapidly prototype operational images. They technologize their solutions by developing programmatic steps to achieve them. In other words, they begin with the current operations and culminate in new and more productive operations.

Let us put individual processing into the perspective of the learning sciences. Almost everything we learn is ultimately incorporated as conditioned responses. What this means is that once we incorporate the conditioned responses we have learned, no real processing occurs between the stimulus input and the conditioned response. We are simply conditioned to make reflex responses.

Today, management is dominated by participative, discriminative thinkers and learners. Armed with repertoires of conditioned responses, they make discriminations with their elaborate branching systems. However, no matter how elaborate their branching discriminations, when the latter are reduced, what remain are only hierarchies of conditioned responses.

The only truly productive processors are the generative processors. Armed with repertoires of generative processes, they generate entirely new and powerful responses. Moreover, they increasingly dedicate their generative processes toward the acquisition of more powerful processing systems.

In individual processing or thinking, we process with the phenomena. This means we have merged with the phenomena and have represented them. To process, we must apply generative processing systems as scaled in Table 4-9 and detailed below:

- **Goaling** by measuring values,

- **Analyzing** by dissembling entities,

- **Synthesizing** by assembling new entities,

- **Operationalizing** by prototyping new entities,

- **Technologizing** by producing the new entities.

Table 4-9. Individual Processing Systems

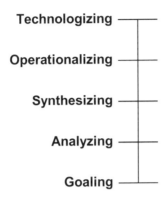

Technologizing

Operationalizing

Synthesizing

Analyzing

Goaling

Individual processing systems enable us to process phenomena by goaling our values; by analyzing our current operations; by synthesizing new and more powerful operations; by operationalizing new objectives; by technologizing new programs (see Figure 4-7). Synthesizing is the key to generative processing. In synthesizing, we expand and then narrow alternative operations. To do this, we insert the models that we developed in information representing. These models enable us to consider the multitude of interactions of operations. The success of all processing is contingent upon the quality of models with which we synthesize new operations.

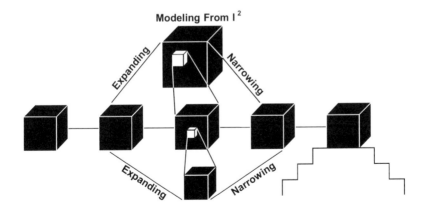

Figure 4-7. Individual Processing Incorporates Information Representing

In short, dimensionalized information is transformed into still more robust and productive information by generative individual processing: goaling (G), analyzing (A), synthesizing (S), operationalizing (O), technologizing (T)—or GASOT (see Figure 4-8). The response (R^2) is transformed into new and more productive responses (R^3) by GASOT.

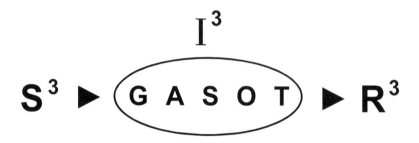

Figure 4-8. Individual Processing Systems

In the final analysis, the power of I^3 is a function of the comprehensiveness of the new capital development systems with which we expand and narrow our alternatives.

In addition, ongoing information relating systems and information representing systems contribute both developmentally and cumulatively to elevate communication for processing purposes. In essence, operational and dimensional information-building continue to elevate our understanding of the complexity and power of the phenomena. In so doing, individual processing prepares us for interpersonal processing: the skills to process interpersonally in an organizational context.

I^4—Interpersonal Processing Systems

Processing is, fourthly, a social science. With the brainpower of others skilled in interpersonal processing, phenomena can grow. In interpersonal processing we join with phenomena in a *process-to-process* dialogue to reach a *critical mass* of processing. It is this critical mass which reveals the principles of growth for both us and phenomena.

Let us put interpersonal processing into the perspective of the social sciences. So-called experts have espoused many different kinds of interpersonal-relating approaches in management. Basically, these approaches are either (1) authoritarian, or manager-centered, (2) employee-, or customer-, centered, or (3) situation-centered. The truth is this: ***none of these relate!***

The authoritarian approach assumes the critical expertise of the manager. With the spiraling changes that are taking place, this is rare. Indeed, as a general rule, expertise is a function of dedication and concentration. And more often than not, the expertise is found in someone else's brainpower. We call this authoritarian approach *"Give and Go!"* The managers *give* the orders, and the employees *go*—attempt to perform them. Even when the manager has expertise, this approach is problematic because the parties involved never get an opportunity to agree upon the tasks.

The employee-centered approach, on the other hand, assumes that critical expertise is in the other person. We call this approach *"Get and Go!"* The managers *get* the direction from employees, who *go* on to perform the tasks. Even when other people have the expertise, they do not benefit from the manager's perspectives in relaying the unit's requirements for performing the tasks.

We label our interpersonal-processing approach *"Get, Give, Grow."*

- First, we *get* the images of others.

- Next, we *give* our images.

- Then, we process to *grow* or *generate* new images.

This is true interpersonal processing: sharing images before generating new images.

In interpersonal processing, processing grows to a critical mass, interactively bridging *neuronal gaps* in all participants by generating insights that were previously unavailable. The possibilities manager is now empowered to invest more enlightened resources in future *developmental mergers*.

Interpersonal processing systems are scaled in Table 4-10 and detailed below:

- **Goaling** by measuring values,
- **Getting** by responding to others' images of entities,
- **Giving** by initiating our images of entities,
- **Growing** by generating new images of entities,
- **Going** by acting to develop new entities.

Table 4-10. Interpersonal Processing Systems

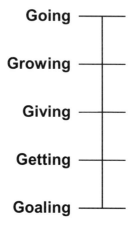

Interpersonal processing systems enable us to process phenomena interpersonally by goaling interpersonally; by *"getting"* the others' images; by *"giving"* our own images; by *"growing"* new images; by *"going"* on to implement the new images. As shown in Figure 4-9, interpersonal processing incorporates individual processing. After sharing images, the people *"grow"* or process interpersonally to generate new and more powerful images.

It is to be emphasized that the productive participants in interpersonal processing are ones who qualified by generating their own individual images. That is the contribution of interpersonal processing: *"ego-free"* processing by representatives of different phenomenal images.

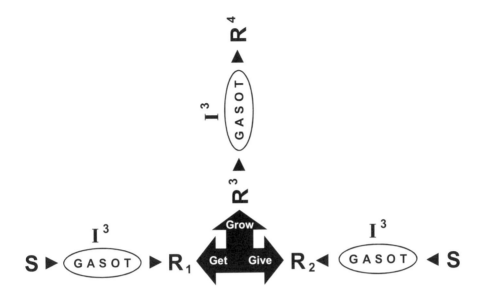

Figure 4-9. Interpersonal Processing Incorporates Individual Processing

The purpose of interpersonal processing is to leverage the potentially multiplicative effects of the processing of multiple individuals (see Figure 4-10). In short, we find that interpersonal processing, used facilitatively, compounds the effect of individual processing. What one can do, more can do much better! This is because empowered people have *"a better process."*

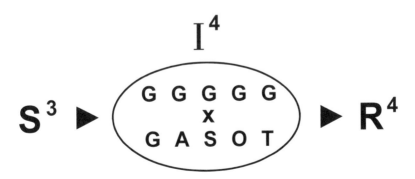

Figure 4-10. Interpersonal Processing Systems

I⁵—Interdependent Processing Systems Skills

Processing is, finally, a science of phenomenology. *Phenomenology* means phenomenal perspective: being able to see phenomena in their various relationships. When our perspective becomes more expansive, we see more and more of the interdependent conditions within which any entity operates. We see relationships to larger and larger entities. When our perspective narrows, we see less and less context but more and more details. The details give us more information about the operations of our subject under study. We come to understand the performance measures or standards by which we operate.

For the possibilities manager, then, interdependent processing is about processing with perspective. Operationally, this means we enter the phenomenon to merge with it. We are dedicated interdependently to discharging its functions by components enabled by processes.

It means expanding our perspective to understand the conditions within which any phenomena operate: they supply the answer to why the phenomena exist. Without perspective, we are lost in a *"micro-dot."* With perspective, we are empowered to see the phenomena for what they are and for what they might become.

It also means generating a perspective on the standards by which we measure performance. Standards are a mix of the uniformity of current performance and the diversity of future performance. Each will change the other. Both will be measured on indices of changeability.

Interdependent processing is the culminating stage in processing. We must now develop images of the continuously changing conditions within which the phenomena operate, as well as images of the continuously changing standards that are generated within the phenomena. The goal of interdependent processing, then, is to develop continuously changing perspectives of phenomenal possibilities.

Perspective educates us about the vectors, or forces, that are acting upon the phenomena. For example, an overview of NCD areas is an interdependent perspective to be processed with. This

136

perspective of *nested* capital development systems may be scaled as shown in Table 4-11 and below:

- **MCD**—Marketplace capital development,
- **OCD**—Organizational capital development,
- **HCD**—Human capital development,
- **ICD**—Information capital development,
- **mCD**—Mechanical capital development.

**Table 4-11. Interdependent Processing Systems
(New Capital Development Systems)**

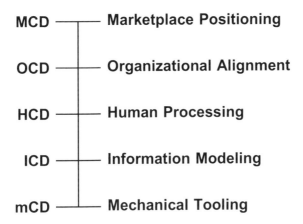

Interdependent processing systems enable us to process phenomena interdependently, discharging phenomenal functions by way of phenomenal components enabled by phenomenal processes (see Figure 4-11). Thus we live and process inside the phenomena we have generated. As illustrated below, we also incorporate interpersonal and individual processing systems to innovate within the phenomena. That is the contribution of interdependent processing:

Interpersonal processing empowered by individual processing dedicated to new and more powerful images of phenomenal dimensions.

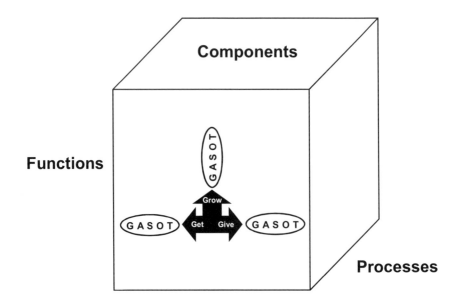

**Figure 4-11. Interdependent Processing Incorporates
Interpersonal and Individual Processing**

In summary, the purpose of interdependent processing is to relate interdependently to phenomena, their conditions, and their standards of performance. Possibilities people express it this way:

> *We become **one** with the phenomena, but more
> than that, we become **multiple** with the changing
> phenomenal experiences.*

Everything is changeably and interdependently related to everything else and all things—including ourselves. The basic principle of interdependent processing is that ***everything is interdependent and changeable***. Are we willing to elevate our processes to relate to our changing, interdependent world?

We process interdependently by bringing our interpersonal and individual processing into interaction with our phenomenal perspective (see Figure 4-12).

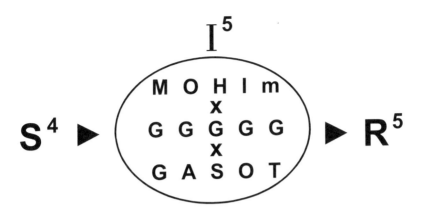

Figure 4-12. Interdependent Processing Systems

We do not culminate our interdependent processing until, figuratively, we become the phenomena themselves and process with their phenomenal systems. We live in the perspective we generate. But, we must keep attuned to the changing nature of nature, process interdependently with it, and modify our perspectives. Phenomena are changeable, and so must be our perspective.

MANAGING HCD

In the Carkhuff Group, we believe that human processing is the heart of managing possibilities. Accordingly, we ask our managers to bring their I^5 **skills** to bear upon all of their management practices. We also believe that human processing is the most powerfully leveraged of all processing systems. This is simply because the human brain is capable of conceiving of anything and everything. It can even generate its own, new neuronal structures. Accordingly, we have developed our HCD management systems in tandem with our possibilities management systems to guide the transformation of our human resources into human capital. Human capital development, or HCD, emphasizes human processing. What makes humans *"capital,"* then, is their processing ability. We label this ability "I^5." HCD may be measured and managed as illustrated in Table 4-12. As may be noted, the "I^5" are, themselves, discriminated at five different levels:

- L1—Detractor, or depressive performance;
- L2—Observer, or subtractive performance;
- L3—Participant, or adequate performance— interchangeable with requirements;
- L4—Contributor, or additive performance;
- L5—Leader, or exemplary performance.

Table 4-12. HCD Management Areas of HCD

LEVELS OF HCD	AREAS OF HCD				
	I^1	I^2	I^3	I^4	I^5
5 - Leader	Standards	Multi-D	Technologizing	Going	Marketplace
4 - Contributor	Conditions	*Nested*-D	Operationalizing	Generating	Organization
3 - Participant	Processes	3D	Synthesizing	Giving	Human
2 - Observer	Components	2D	Analyzing	Getting	Information
1 - Detractor	Functions	1D	Goaling	Goaling	Mechanical

Thus, levels of "I^5" may be measured by the skills involved:

- I^1 by FCPCS—Functions, Components, Processes, Conditions, Standards;
- I^2 by 1, 2, 3, ND, MD—1D, 2D, 3D, *Nested*-D, Multi-D;
- I^3 by GASOT—Goaling, Analyzing, Synthesizing, Operationalizing, Technologizing;
- I^4 by GGGGG—Goaling, Getting, Giving, Generating, Going;
- I^5 by MOHIm—MCD, OCD, HCD, ICD, mCD.

Most people do not reach the level of participant. To function at Level 3, or the participant level, most people require training in:

- Information relating through processes;

- Information representing with 3D models;

- Individual processing by synthesizing information;

- Interpersonal processing by giving images;

- Interdependent processing with human phenomena.

To become contributing human capital, people must function at Level 4. For some people, this means intensive training and reinforcing applications in:

- Information relating by conditions;

- Information representing with *nested* dimensional modeling;

- Individual processing by operationalizing information;

- Interpersonal processing by generating with others to create new images;

- Interdependent processing with organizational phenomena.

Finally, to become leaders or exemplary human capital, people must function at Level 5. For some few, this means new modeling and performance opportunities in:

- Information relating by standards;

- Information representing with multidimensional modeling;

- Individual processing by technologizing information;

- Interpersonal processing by going on to plan the achievement of new images;

- Interdependent processing with marketplace phenomena.

These levels of performance may be further distinguished by measurable indices, as shown in Table 4-13. As we can see, the **detractors** tend not to discharge their tasks on either quantitative or qualitative indices. Their volume, rate, and timeliness are essentially unrecorded. Their products or services, nurtured to completion only through the painstaking efforts of others, are inaccurate, dysfunctional, and inappropriate. The customer usually ends up rejecting the products or services for a variety of reasons.

Table 4-13. Indices of Performance

CUSTOMER

EMPLOYEES	PRODUCTS AND SERVICES						BENEFITS
	QUANTITY			QUALITY			
	Volume	Rate	Timeliness	Accuracy	Functional	Initiative	
5 — Leaders	Superior	Superior	Before Time	Finely Detailed	Highly Functional	Break-through	Empirical Documentation
4 — Contributors	High	High	Before Time	Accurate	Functional	Modifications	Customer Satisfaction
3 — Participants	On Target	On Target	On Time	On Standard	Usable	Programmatic	Customer Reception
2 — Observers	Low	Low	Late	Lacks Detail	Problematic	None	Customer Changes
1 — Detractors	None	None	Never	Totally Inaccurate	Dysfunctional	Inappropriate	Customer Rejection

The **observers**, in turn, are low in the volume and rate, and late in the timeliness of their products and services. Their products usually lack the details needed to complete them and are only problematically functional. The customer usually returns the products for significant changes or alterations.

The **participants** are usually on target on five of the indices: volume, rate, timeliness, accuracy, and functionality. If the organization has programmed enough options into its standard operating procedures, then the participants may sometimes "appear" to be initiative as well. Accordingly, the customers receive or accept the products or services.

The **contributors** are high in volume and rate, and before time with their products and services. Their products are accurate and functional, and they make useful modifications to satisfy the customer.

142

Finally, the **leaders** are superior in volume, rate, and timeliness. Their products are finely detailed, highly functional, and highly initiative. They are able to document customer benefits empirically.

Clearly, the only true human capital are those who function at the highest levels and deliver the greatest benefits. In this regard, the **detractors** are *"depressor variables"* who actually depress the contributions of others to high-level performance. Dominated as they are by conditioned responding, they are useful only transitionally in a labor pool awaiting replacement by automation.

The **observers**, in turn, are a *"disappearing species."* While discriminative learning is required for most purposes, it is insufficient in and of itself. The best that we can say about observers is that discriminative learning is necessary but not sufficient for human capitalization. Moreover, observers tend to narrow the contributions of generators to the point where they are trivialized.

The **participants** are the threshold of human capital. Empowered by generative processing systems, they can keep pace with, or exceed, or even create, the spiraling changes in requirements. This will soon become the base line of functioning in the Age of Ideation.

The **contributors** are those who, in addition to their engaging in generative processing systems, are aligned with organizational processing systems. Thus, guided by organizational functions, they generate new images "directionfully."

Finally, the **leaders** are in tune with the requirements of the marketplace as well as the capabilities of their organizations. Empowered by positioning perspective, leaders set in motion generative marketplace systems that, in turn, initiate other processing systems. Ultimately, the leadership level of functioning will be required of all possibilities managers.

We need only view ourselves as managers in order to discriminate our personal requirements. Our conditioned responding and discriminative learning systems are no longer adequate to meet twenty-first-century requirements. Generative human processing is a minimal requirement for participation as a manager in the global marketplace. Organizational processing empowers us to be contributors to organizational profitability. Marketplace processing empowers us to be leaders in the generation of new wealth.

Human capital is defined by I^5 skills for performance:

- I^1—Information relating to define phenomenal operations;
- I^2—Information representing to dimensionalize images of phenomena;
- I^3—Individual processing to generate new images of phenomena;
- I^4—Interpersonal processing to generate more powerful images of phenomena;
- I^5—Interdependent processing to generate the most powerful images of phenomena.

This is true human capital![*]

IN TRANSITION

The power of the HCD model is indeed remarkable. As we can see in Figure 4-13, the model enables continuous interdependent processing in implementing continuous organizational alignment. With our understanding of this model, we are positioned to consider ICD, or information capital development—the subject of our next chapter.

In summary, human capital development emphasizes generating possibilities. By transforming phenomena into operations! By representing phenomena individually! By processing phenomena! By processing interpersonally with phenomena! By processing interdependently with phenomenal conditions! By processing all of these stages simultaneously and synergistically!

---

[*] The I^5 operations are fully developed in Carkhuff and Berenson's *The Possibilities Leader—The New Science of Possibilities Management*, HRD Press, 2000.

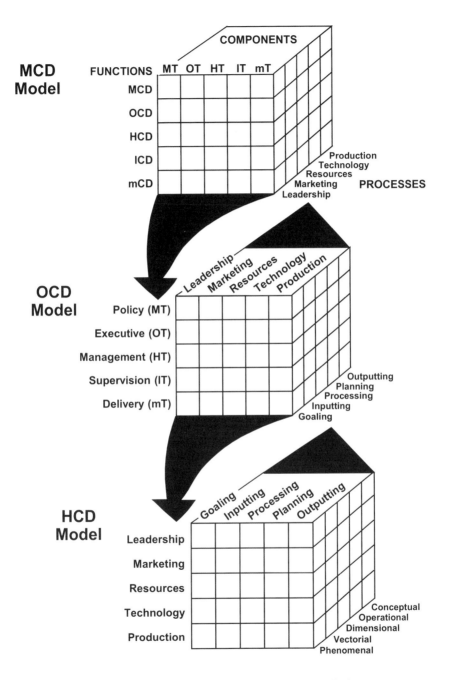

Figure 4-13. MCD–OCD–HCD Models

145

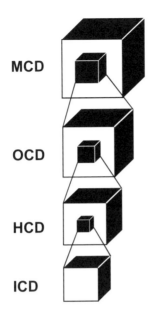

MCD

OCD

HCD

ICD

5 Managing Information Capital Development

Information modeling is the synergistic partner of human processing.

"What Now?"
—The Power of ICD

Our client was already at work applying the knowledge-management tools of the 1990s: assigning knowledge collectors and writers to post learnings and relevant information; building web pages, intranet and Internet bulletin boards and chat rooms; providing 800 numbers, help desks, and so on. The culminating product of these efforts was the ongoing collection and dissemination of corporate knowledge in the form of multiple corporate-knowledge databases.

These knowledge-management efforts were highly successful. Corporate knowledge was finally widely available for internal use as well as for customers, suppliers, vendors, and partners. No more scrambling for knowledge that should have been available in the first place. Our client concluded, "With our current approach to knowledge management, we are, for the moment, ahead of our competitors. It won't be long, however, before everyone automates to manage knowledge as we have done. We realize that our competitive edge will soon be eroded."

With knowledge management fast becoming a business requirement and no longer serving as a source of competitive advantage, our client asked us, "What now? *'Information Capital'?* Sounds intriguing. What is it? How do we manage its development? How do we upgrade from knowledge management to ICD management?"

Relying upon our research in defining and relating ICD, we set out to enable the organization to elevate its information practices from the management of "common knowledge" to the ongoing creation of information capital. Specifically, our goal was to help our client organization install a process for generating and managing new ICD databases. Our methods would include IC mining, ICD aligning, and IC linking strategies.

ICD Mining

Using the client's corporate-knowledge databases as stimulus, we turned our attention to the generative sources of this information—our client's employees. We knew that people could not be expected to produce ICD without first being empowered with the necessary ICD development skills. We empowered them with training in I^5 interdependent processing skills and asked them to apply these skills to *mine* the knowledge they already had. We asked them to use their new skills to model their ideas in new ways. The ICD mining process involved building upon conceptual and operational information to develop scaled, dimensional information. This process resulted in new ICD as people scaled their information and defined their scales both in terms of "what-is" and "what-could-be." This new information was more robust in its value to users, since the processes of dimensionalizing information involve thoughtful analysis and synthesis of information. The result of ICD mining was a higher quality of information. Complete with explanations and examples, the employees created scaled ICD databases (see Figure 5-1) and the start of comprehensive ICD databases.

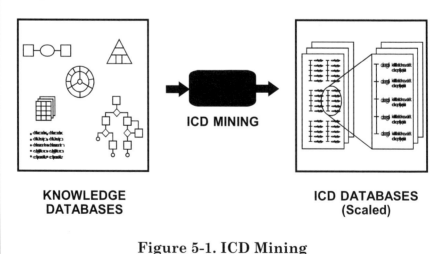

KNOWLEDGE DATABASES

ICD MINING

ICD DATABASES (Scaled)

Figure 5-1. ICD Mining

ICD Aligning

We then coached and supported our client to align the organization's ICD scales. These explicit scales presented information in a form that juxtaposed one scale with another. The process of ICD alignment involves considerable negotiation among ICD owners as to how and why particular ICD scales could or should be aligned. This alignment process was highly generative, resulting in requirements for new thinking, new information, new information alignment, and, ultimately, new corporate initiatives. The outputs of ICD alignment were still more comprehensive ICD databases—scaled and aligned databases (see Figure 5-2).

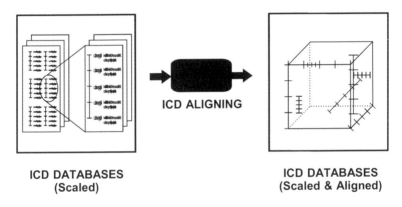

ICD DATABASES
(Scaled)

ICD ALIGNING

ICD DATABASES
(Scaled & Aligned)

Figure 5-2. ICD Aligning

ICD Linking

Finally, we worked with our client's people to help them apply their I[5] skills to build linked databases. This process included linking all forms of ICD that were judged by our client as useful: lists of data elements, tables, matrices, systems and workflow drawings, 3D models, *nested* models, and many new, creative, and highly communicative information representations.

ICD linking involves generating "electronic threads" to ease both push and pull information access. The results of this process were new scaled, aligned, and linked ICD databases (see Figure 5-3).

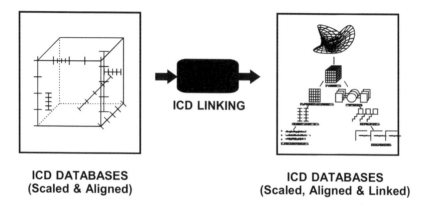

ICD DATABASES
(Scaled & Aligned)

ICD LINKING

ICD DATABASES
(Scaled, Aligned & Linked)

Figure 5-3. ICD Linking

ICD Management

The new twenty-first-century ICD databases retained links to the lower-level information originally captured in the 1990s knowledge management systems. The knowledge management systems had kept our client, in a competitive sense, *even*— merely able to supply employees, customers, suppliers, and partners with what had now become "common knowledge."

The new ICD databases held highly leveraged ICD, the result of generative and innovative thinking required by the ICD management processes of mining, aligning, and linking (see Figure 5-4). Now our client has the renewed and ongoing competitive advantage that comprehensive ICD management delivers.

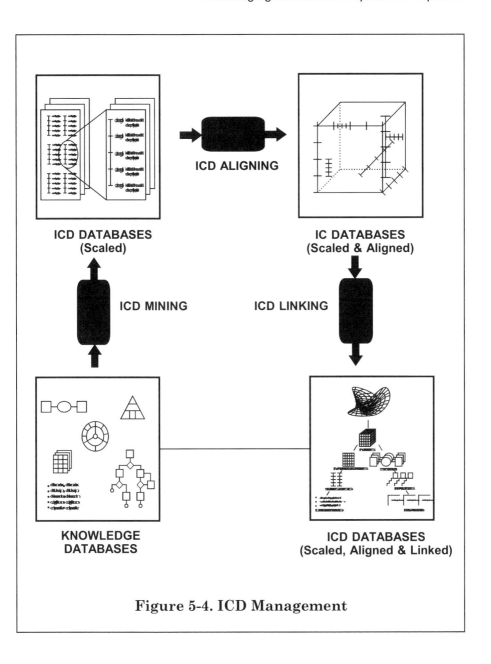

Figure 5-4. ICD Management

Information—nations treasure it. The marketplace requires it. Corporations generate it. Managers manage it. Yet no one seems to be able to define it clearly! In businesses we speak about information by using terms like "knowledge management"; but aside from our inventory and transaction databases, most of our files are filled with lots of reports and memos—often of little or no value. In fact, this wordy excess is a depressor variable for our productivity. We pay too much attention to it! Relatedly, while we promote the rapidity of our information *"connectivity"* capabilities, we still have little idea of how to develop and model valuable information to communicate across our networks. So what is information? How can we define and so develop and manage this information that everyone acknowledges as critical for economic growth?

To orient ourselves to defining information, let us begin by defining a few of the words that are used to describe it:

- **"Information"** is derived from the verb, "to inform." It implies *modeling knowledge* of the operational nature of phenomena. Information communicates operations: what something is, how it works, what it does, when and where it does what it does, and why it does it.

- **"Knowledge,"** in turn, is derived from the verb, "to know." It implies a conceptual understanding of the nature of phenomena and their relationships.

- **"Modeling"** is derived from the verb, "to model." It implies imaging, representing, or displaying the multidimensional nature of phenomena.

Now let us put these definitions together: *Information involves modeling to display images of the multidimensional relationships of phenomena.* This is a summary of the current state of defining information. It is helpful only if it starts us thinking about information.

This chapter will present an introduction to what we call *information capital development,* or *ICD. ICD* will empower us to develop and model information.

MODELING INFORMATION

We may build a model of information capital by representing the functions, or intentions, of information; its components, or parts; and its transformation processes, or how these information components service these functions. The functions are defined by what the information is intended to accomplish. The components of information are defined by their ingredients and how these ingredients are related. The processes of information are defined as the methods that can be applied to transform one form of information into another and so serve the intended purposes of information.

A three-dimensional model has been developed for representing the functions, components, and processes of information. This model will serve us in our responsibilities to develop and manage information. We label our model of information "ICD," or "information capital development." Building it involves four general steps:

1. Scaling the functions, or intentions, of information;

2. Scaling the components of information that will service these functions;

3. Scaling the transformational processes that may be applied to change information so it can complete its responsibilities;

4. Representing the interaction of these elements of ICD in a three-dimensional model or figure.

This chapter will provide a demonstration of how to carry out these steps.

Once we understand how to model ICD, we will be able to manage our information-modeling responsibilities by using our ICD model. We will begin to manage our information by asking ourselves to scale our information. We will cross information components with information functions to develop matrices of information. By bringing these into interaction with a third scale, the transformation processes of the information, we will develop three-dimensional models of information capital. Scaling, matrixing, and modeling are useful methods for developing and managing information.

157

Our model building will help us answer critical questions about information building and knowledge management. Those questions include:

- *How do we generate and represent information?*

- *What are our current methods and policies regarding information modeling and knowledge management?*

- *What current practices are effective?*

- *What are we missing?*

- *Is our information modeled and available?*

- *Are our various forms of information related?*

- *Are our standards of performance in information capital development and knowledge management aligned with the expectations and requirements of our customers?*

The growth and life of our information, our human initiatives, and our organizations are dependent upon our answers to these questions.

Scaling Human Functions

The functions of information are to service people. Another way to say this is that the purpose of information is to serve the human processing. To describe the functions of information, we look to our human capital development (HCD) model. As shown in Table 5-1, we derive the functions of information from the components of our HCD model: goaling, or valuing; inputting, or analyzing; processing, or synthesizing; planning, or operationalizing; and outputting, or technologizing. As may be noted, the functions of information are human functions.

This scale of information functions is a useful initial *map-in* to orient us to the intentions of information capital. Further analyses of each level of these functions will provide a deeper understanding and a more clearly defined description of the specific intentions we may have for our information. As we learn more about each of these levels of requirements for human processing, or thinking, we will further define the functions of information.

Table 5-1. Human Functions

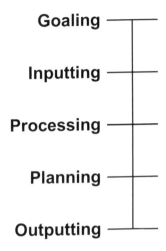

By defining the functions of information, we begin to see the imbedded requirements. Does the information serve the processes of human thinking? If not, then our information is useless and we should stop collecting it and distributing it. If our information does service thinking, then we need to take a closer look at its component parts and the quality of these representations.

Scaling Information Components

In this step of modeling ICD, we define information components, or ingredients. (Later sections in this chapter will explain what we mean by these components.) As we may recall in viewing Table 5-2, these information components were previously introduced as processes in our HCD model. They are as follows:

- **Conceptual,** or verbal, information;
- **Operational,** or systems, information;
- **Dimensional,** or modeled, information;

- **Vectorial,** or facsimile *"force,"* information;
- **Phenomenal,** or naturalistic *"source,"* information.

Table 5-2. Information Components

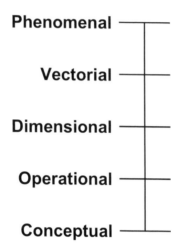

Phenomenal

Vectorial

Dimensional

Operational

Conceptual

This scale of information components is a useful initial *map-in* for analyzing the quality of our information. Further analyses of each of these types of information will provide us with a more detailed description of the kinds of information we need to develop.

By defining the components of information, we have tools for analyzing the quality of information. Do our information representations best serve their intentions? If not, then we should consider transforming those representations into other forms of component information.

Information Capital Matrix

We begin to see the value of modeling our information when we represent information components, or ingredients, in relation to their functions. We do this by creating what we call the Information Capital Matrix (see Table 5-3). This matrix presents us with a visual model of how information components are aligned to discharge multiple levels of human intentions.

Table 5-3. Information Capital Matrix

ICD COMPONENTS

HCD FUNCTIONS	Phenomenal	Vectorial	Dimensional	Operational	Conceptual
Goaling					
Inputting					
Processing					
Planning					
Outputting					

With the Information Capital Matrix, we begin to see the distribution of our information and its intentions. The matrix should stimulate many important questions about the quality and availability of the information that we have or need in order to service the processes of human performance. With this window on our information, we may begin to build our *"information capital."*

Scaling Mechanical Processes

The next step in building our ICD model is to introduce the mechanical processes that enable the information components to discharge human intentions. (Later, in Chapter 6, we will take a closer look at these processes.) As we can see in Table 5-4, they include transformation processes for the following:

- Changing the **functions,** or responsibilities or outputs, of the phenomena;

- Changing the **components,** or parts or inputs, of the phenomena;

- Changing the **processes,** or transforming procedures, of the phenomena;

- Changing the **conditions,** or contexts or environments, of the phenomena;

- Changing the **standards,** or measures of achievement, of the phenomena.

These processes of information transformation provide the final piece of our model of ICD.

Table 5-4. Mechanical Processes

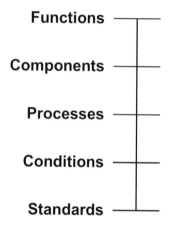

ICD Model

We complete our ICD model by adding the processes of information transformation (see Figure 5-5). The objective of the ICD model may be succinctly expressed in this way:

> *The functions, or intentions, of human processing are discharged by information components enabled by mechanical processes.*

In other words, the mCD processes enable the ICD components to discharge HCD functions.

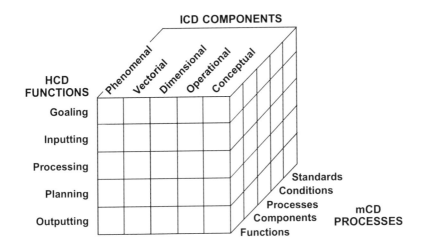

Figure 5-5. ICD Model

We begin information capital analysis and development by scaling, matrixing, and modeling our information using the ICD model. Once we have modeled our current information, we will analyze its quality and availability. Without a comprehensive understanding of information capital, we are missing huge opportunities for developing and aligning the information needed to grow our organizations. With an understanding of information capital, we may elevate the performance of our human capital to maximize its contributions within the context of our aligned and marketplace-positioned organizations.

Next, we will focus upon better understanding "information" so we may improve our processes for modeling and managing our *information capital,* and for developing it as the powerful source of wealth that it can become.

PROCESSES FOR INFORMATION MODELING

Before we can engage in meaningful information modeling and productive knowledge management, we must expand our understanding about information beyond vague generalities. This involves defining the components of information capital to include the following:

- **Conceptual information** for representing relationships between phenomena,

- **Operational information** for representing phenomenal operations,

- **Dimensional information** for representing the dimensions of phenomena,

- **Vectorial information** for representing the forces and directions of phenomena,

- **Phenomenal information** for representing the sources of the phenomena themselves.

By building these types of information, we may model and manage our information-modeling responsibilities.

Conceptual Information

By definition, *conceptual information states the relationship between things.* The value of conceptual knowledge is to state the relationships within, between, and among words or numbers or other schematic representations.

The levels of conceptual information are illustrated in Table 5-5. These levels have simple verbal definitions:

- **Facts** are the identification *labels* we attach to phenomena.

- **Concepts** *state* the *relationships* within or between phenomena.

- **Principles** *explain* these *relationships* within or between phenomena.

- **Applications** specify the *contexts* in which the phenomena are demonstrated.

- **Objectives** specify the *standards,* or the measures of performance, of these demonstrations of phenomena.

Table 5-5. Levels of Conceptual Information

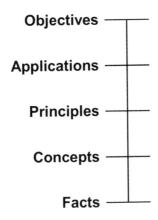

Objectives

Applications

Principles

Concepts

Facts

Conceptual information is the simplest form of information modeling. We use conceptual information when we *verbally* define phenomena: things (facts) have relationships (concepts) which are explained (principles) in contexts (applications) so that we can accomplish demonstrations (objectives).

Most of our information is represented conceptually. For example, facts and concepts fill our e-mails. When this information is further developed, we may write or read sentences that explain how certain facts are related. We may describe information about applications, or contexts, to tell when and where and perhaps why something is so. We may write or read information about standards of performance and why these standards are so.

Again, conceptual information is verbal—it is a string of sentences. It may be informative and useful but also difficult. An accurate, comprehensive report may be useful but require a lot of effort to write and a lot of effort to read.

Operational Information

Operational information defines phenomena by their operations, or systems parts. We say that we have defined our information operationally when we have defined the phenomena's systems operations. In comparing this type of information to

conceptual, we find that *conceptual information* **describes relationships,** whereas *operational information* **defines the operations (systems parts) involved in the relationships.**
The levels of operational information are defined by their operations, or systems parts, as shown below. Operational information can be collected or generated by answering these basic questions:

- **Functions**—**What** are we trying to do?

- **Components**—**Who** or **what** is involved?

- **Processes**—**How** are we doing it?

- **Conditions**—**Why** we are doing it, and **when** and **where** are we doing it?

- **Standards**—**Why** we are doing it this way, and **how well** are we doing it?

In practice, operational information may be applied as follows:

- **Functions**—The products or services intended as outputs;

- **Components**—The parts or participants involved as inputs;

- **Processes**—The procedures or methods employed for transformation;

- **Conditions**—The contexts or environments of the operations;

- **Standards**—The measures of excellence or achievement for the operations.

When we understand that conceptual information can be defined with operational terms, we are able to transform and redefine facts, concepts, principles, applications, and objectives by their operations, or systems parts. A matrix that communicates how conceptual and operational information is related is presented in Figure 5-6.

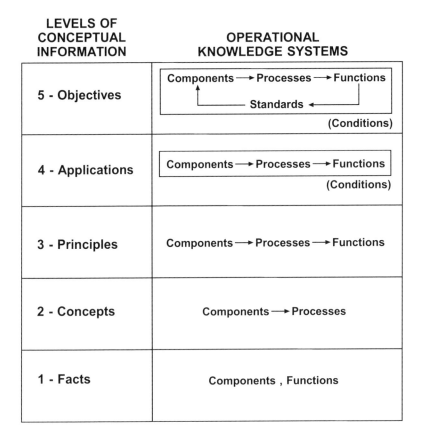

Figure 5-6. Operational Definitions of Knowledge

As can be seen, by redefining conceptual information by operational systems, we have now redefined the conceptual information as developmental and cumulative. This means that:

- Facts are incorporated by concepts;

- Concepts are incorporated by principles;

- Principles are included in applications;

- Applications are incorporated by objectives.

Conceptual information, then, is translated into operational information as follows:

167

- **Facts** are conceptually represented and generally understood as the labels we attach to things. Operationally defined, facts are the specific components and functions involved. Facts tell what we have done or what we are trying to do (functions) and who or what is involved (components).

- **Concepts** describe relationships within or between phenomena. Operationally defined, concepts are the relationships within and between components and/or functions: between components and components; between functions and functions; between components and functions. For ICD purposes, concepts describe which parts and participants (components) are related to which intentions (functions).

- **Principles** are explanations of the relationships within or between phenomena. Operationally defined, principles systematically explain the relationship of components and functions as well as the intervening processes involved. Principles include the steps (processes) that the parts and participants (components) will take to accomplish their intentions (functions).

- **Applications** include information about the contexts in which phenomena are demonstrated. Operationally defined, applications are described as systems of components, processes, and functions along with conditions or systems boundaries. Applications information tells when and where (conditions) the principles will be applied.

- **Objectives** are conceptual statements of standards, or measures of performance. Operationally defined, objectives are described as systems of components, processes, functions, and conditions along with information about measures of performance. Objectives tell how well (standards) the applications need to be performed.

Let us consider the differences between conceptual and operational information.

Communication with conceptual information is the medium of conversation. It is also the medium of poets and novelists. We hear and read many interacting pieces of conceptual information, but it is left to our brainpower to put the pieces together. Hopefully, finally, we may have an "Ah, ha!" experience. Conceptual conversations and reading can be highly rewarding. They are critical to relationship building and may stimulate our thinking, however inefficiently.

In business, with customers paying for our time, we must be both effective and efficient in our communications. If we are not, our customers will become our former customers. By building information that is operational, by its systems parts, we cut through "all those words." Basically, we discipline ourselves to develop our information in terms of systems: functions, or outputs; components, or inputs; processes, or procedures; conditions, or systems boundaries; and standards, or measures for performance feedback.

How do we represent this operational information? It is most efficient to represent operational information in systems drawings (see Figure 5-7). Wouldn't we be pleased if people who worked with or for us developed and delivered systems drawings to us? These drawings take the meandering string of words out of documents. With operational systems drawings we may now get to what people do best—thinking about how they may change and improve upon systems operations.

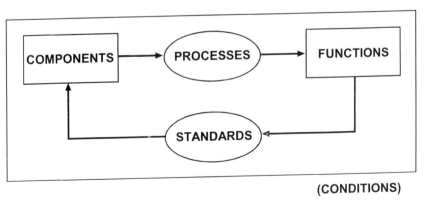

Figure 5-7. Operational Systems Drawing

This does not mean that written sentences and paragraphs no longer have a place in business communications. They still do: for example, when they explain systems drawings or when they give "color commentary" to operational information.

Remember, **conceptual information** is *verbal*—it is a string of sentences. It answers the basic interrogatives. It requires a lot of effort to write and to read.

Operational information is *systems information*. We may represent it in a systems drawing or describe it in a series of sentences that focus on the operations of a system or systems.

Dimensional Information

What is dimensional information? From an operational systems perspective, we may say that each operation (system part) is a dimension of information. From this perspective then, there are five dimensions to any system: functions, or outputs; components, or inputs; processes, or procedures; conditions, or systems boundaries; and standards, or feedback measures. Dimensional information presents this operational systems information as lists or scales; matrices or tables; models; *nested* models; and multidimensional *nested* models. The levels of dimensional information are defined by the complexity and nature of their dimensionality:

- 1D—**One-dimensional** list or scale,

- 2D—**Two-dimensional** matrix or table,

- 3D—**Three-dimensional** model,

- ND—*Nested*-**dimensional** models,

- MD—**Multidimensional** *nested* models.

We are all familiar with one-dimensional lists. Many of us know about some forms of scaling. Some of us understand two-dimensional matrices or tables. A few of us have been introduced to three-dimensional, *x-y-z* axis modeling. *Nested*-dimensional and multidimensional modeling displays new axes or planes beyond three dimensions (see Figure 5-8).

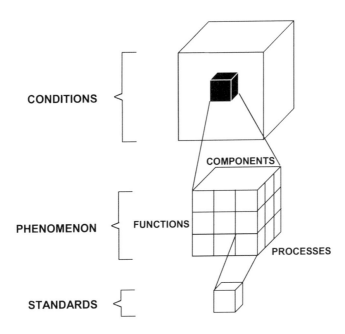

CONDITIONS

COMPONENTS

PHENOMENON — **FUNCTIONS**

PROCESSES

STANDARDS

Figure 5-8. Dimensional Information

We may continue to represent these dimensions with additional three-dimensional models. As shown in Figure 5-8, the 3D model is *nested* in a higher-order model representing conditions. In turn, the 3D model *nests* lower-order models representing standards. All models of higher- and lower-order phenomena have their own dimensionality: functions, components, processes, conditions, standards.

Dimensional information representations are different from operational systems drawings. The lowest levels of dimensional representation, 1D lists or scales and 2D matrices or tables, are used to communicate partial operational systems information. The higher levels of dimensional representations can communicate the interaction of multiple systems. This information provides us with perspectives that are best represented in *nested*-dimensional and multidimensional modeling.

By building dimensional information, we discipline ourselves to develop our information with its multidimensionality in mind. Multidimensional modeling is a tool for communicating invaluable perspective. Wouldn't we be pleased if people who worked with or for us developed and delivered dimensional information to us? Then we could expand and narrow the products of our co-developed ideation by using the tools of dimensional modeling: 1D, 2D, 3D, ND, and MD.

Vectorial Information

Vectors are the forces of phenomena themselves. They exist whether we recognize them or not. In nature, if a tidal wave is approaching land, it is a force on the way whether we realize that force or not. Likewise, in the business environment, if a competitor's breakthrough product is about to be launched and will make our product obsolete, it is a vector about to smash us whether we realize that vector or not.

Vectorial information emphasizes facsimile representations of the actual forces of phenomena upon other phenomena. Vectorial information represents both the *direction* and *magnitude* of these forces. The direction indicates a particular course. The magnitude indicates the power of the force. The direction and magnitude of vectors may be represented by the convergence of forces as illustrated in Figure 5-9.

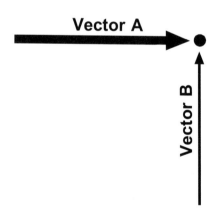

Figure 5-9. Vectorial Forces

In this instance, a phenomenon is about to be impacted by two vectors, or forces. Both of these vectors will soon contribute to defining the context within which the phenomenon operates. As may be noted, Vector A is represented as having considerably greater force than Vector B.

We may also view an example of the effects of the direction and magnitude of vectors upon phenomena (see Figure 5-10). In this instance, the same two vectors are represented as having impacted upon a phenomenon at a certain point. The interaction of these vectors generates a resultant value.

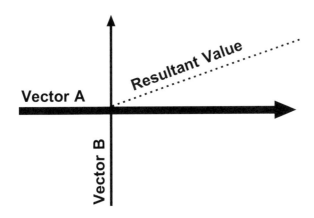

Figure 5-10. Vectorial Forces and Resultant Value

We live in a world of vectorial forces and resultant values. From a defensive business position, we hope that we can see the vectors coming, represent them informationally, and process their impact. From an offensive position, if we can see the vectors and represent them informationally before our competitors do, then opportunities are ours for the taking. From a business perspective, the issues are straightforward: Do we recognize the vectors that impact upon us? Do we represent these vectors informationally so we can impact upon them with intentionality?

In our own work, for example, we have researched the vectors of marketplace positioning, organizational alignment, human processing, information modeling, and mechanical tooling (see Figure 5-11). We define these forces in 3D models that we call *new capital development models* (MCD, OCD, HCD, ICD, mCD). We represent the force and direction of these vectors by the way we have nested them and by arrows that communicate deductive and inductive process movements.

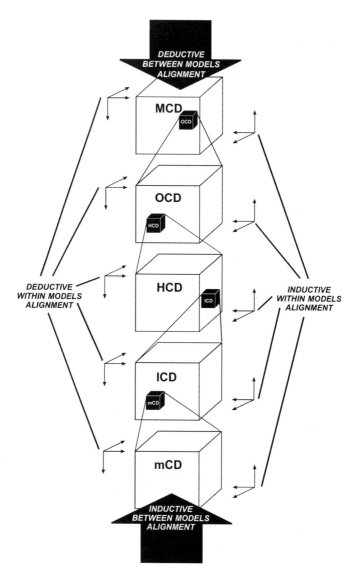

Figure 5-11. Vectorial Perspective

174

As may be noted, the levels of vectorial force and direction are defined by their capital development models:

 Marketplace capital development, or marketplace forces;

 Organizational capital development, or organizational forces;

 Human capital development, or human forces;

 Information capital development, or information forces;

 Mechanical capital development, or mechanical forces.

Certainly, there are many vectors at work in our universe. We present our new capital development systems as an example of our understanding of the powerful vectors at work in our business environments. We hope that these vectors prove to be valuable tools for generating wealth in the twenty-first century and beyond.

Vectorial information involves representations of phenomenal conditions. It is humankind's way of representing the force and direction of nature's phenomena. When we discipline ourselves to seek out vectorial information, we are determined in our search to understand the forces, and the direction of forces, acting upon phenomena. Without this focus, our conceptual, operational, and dimensional information may be inaccurate or irrelevant. When we represent vectors in our information representations, we communicate the contextual forces that are critical to us. With an understanding of vectorial information, we may intervene to enhance phenomena for humankind's purposes.

Phenomenal Information

Phenomenal information is the source of all information.
Scientific relating to phenomena reveals the following shared
characteristics of *all* phenomena:

- Phenomena are inherently **multidimensional:** a
  multitude of curvilinear dimensions interact to define the
  phenomena.

- Phenomena are inherently **interdependent:** the social
  nature of nature asserts that (1) nothing can exist by
  itself, (2) nothing can grow by itself, and (3) nothing can
  live or die by itself.

- Phenomena are inherently **changeable:** the changeable
  nature of nature asserts that all phenomena are continuously changing in qualitative substance as well as
  quantitative form. Phenomena are always moving—
  birthing, growing, relating, dying, being born again.

Each characteristic is a required condition for the other characteristics.

Any generic representation of phenomenal conditions is captured at a *"window of convergence"* occurring at a particular point
in space and time, as represented in Figure 5-12. As may be noted,
multidimensional, interdependent, and changeable phenomena are
represented here in a curvilinear form.

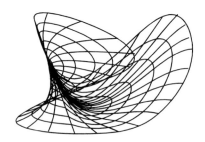

Figure 5-12. Phenomenal Information

A good illustration of phenomenal information in the business arena is the formation of a market *"wave."* The wave may be generated by breakthrough technologies; however, it is formed in the commercial marketplace by the multitude of buying and selling decisions that occur each day in the marketplace.

Another example of phenomenal information is presented in Figure 5-13. In this instance, we (the authors) researched data on the marketplace of mechanical and information technologies. Composed of literally trillions of data points, these phenomena are represented in curvilinear form to help discriminate and communicate them. As illustrated, the mechanical technologies (mT) *"peak"* as a source of comparative advantage around 1960, while the information technologies (IT) *"peak"* around 1980.

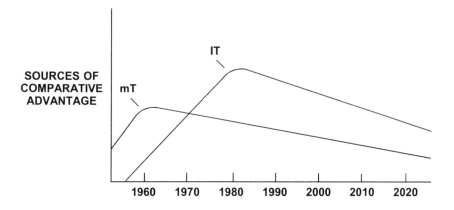

Figure 5-13. Data-Based Curves of Phenomenal Information

In a similar manner, our projected curves, themselves based upon trillions of predicted data points, also illustrate phenomenal modeling. As shown in Figure 5-14, the following technologies rise to become sources of comparative advantage in the marketplace: human technologies (HT), organizational technologies (OT), and marketplace technologies (MT).

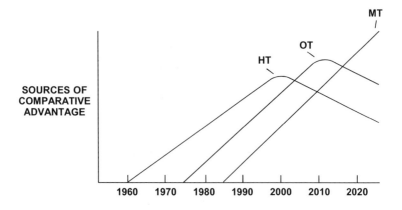

**Figure 5-14. Projected Curves of
Phenomenal Information**

We may derive vectorial models from phenomenal information as illustrated in Figure 5-15. Here, multidimensional models are derived to represent the specific forces, or vectors, that compose the phenomenal curves. As we can see, lower-order technologies are represented by models that are *nested* in higher-order technologies. Such nesting is an example of representing vectors of phenomena acting upon other phenomena. In this instance, the vectors, or forces, of one technology act upon other technologies.

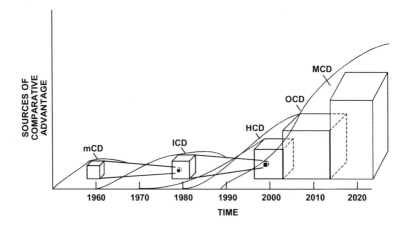

**Figure 5-15. Vectorial Information Derived
From Phenomenal Information**

The significance of phenomenal information is that we begin to comprehend and define phenomenal possibilities. We can begin to understand that the source of all phenomena is the shared characteristic of interdependency. Interdependency is the universal force—the *"seminal process,"* the principle dynamic. It draws its vitality from the social nature of nature.

The human significance of phenomenal information is that we can derive vectorial models to represent the directions and forces of phenomena; we can model our *"universes"* as we understand them to be. Within them, we can attempt to derive the multidimensional, operational, and conceptual information that empowers us develop hypotheses as the basis for interventions of human intentionality.

MANAGING ICD

We may measure and manage ICD as illustrated next in Table 5-6. As may be noted, the areas of new capital development (NCD) information are discriminated by the levels of ICD:

- Conceptual (lexical) levels, where verbal representations of facts, concepts, principles, applications, and objectives are made;

- Operational (systems) levels, where conceptual representations are transformed into operational systems;

- Dimensional (orthogonal) levels, where operational systems representation are transformed into dimensional information: 1D, 2D, 3D, *nested,* and multidimensional modeling;

- Vectorial levels, which are facsimiles of the forces acting upon phenomena and their requirements upon dimensional information and operational systems;

- Phenomenal levels, which represent the phenomena themselves and constitute the conditions within which all other information operates.

Table 5-6. NCD–ICD Management

LEVELS OF ICD	AREAS OF NCD INFORMATION				
	MCD	OCD	HCD	ICD	mcD
Phenomenal					
Vectorial					
Dimensional					
Operational					
Conceptual					

ICD management means discriminating the levels of ICD represented and communicated by our employees in all areas of new capital development. When we build inductively, the lower levels of information—conceptual and operational—have only limited value. When we derive deductively, all levels of information have great value. Interdependent processing requires all levels of ICD.

We may find it helpful to view the management of a subset of ICD. This is illustrated in Table 5-7, for assessments of the levels of HCD information.

Table 5-7. HCD–ICD Management

LEVELS OF ICD	AREAS OF HCD INFORMATION				
	I^1	I^2	I^3	I^4	I^5
Phenomenal					
Vectorial					
Dimensional					
Operational					
Conceptual	When _components . . ._ By _processes . . ._ Then _functions . . ._ So that _conditions . . ._ As measured by _standards_				

In assessing our current levels of HCD information, we might ask questions about what levels of HCD information we have available. For example:

- Is our information about I^1 relating skills...
  - *conceptual?*
  - *operational?*
  - *dimensional?*
  - *vectorial?*
  - *phenomenal?*

- How does our information rate for the HCD skill areas of I^2, I^3, I^4, and I^5?

Our responses to these questions will tell us much about the quality of our HCD information, what we have to manage and what we need to obtain.

IN TRANSITION

ICD is about continuous information modeling to implement continuous interdependent processing (see Figure 5-16). In ICD modeling, ICD components are dedicated to HCD functions and enabled by mCD processes.

Current concepts of *knowledge management*, at best, describe the lowest levels of ICD modeling. At worst, current knowledge-management practices may be *depressor variables* in the equation for generating wealth.

ICD modeling relates to HCD processing in the same manner that HCD processing relates to the OCD organization alignment system. Potentially, every ICD model is useful within every phase of human processing: interrelating, information representing, processing—individually, interpersonally, interdependently. Thus, ICD models are *nested* within *"possibilities processing systems,"* which are *nested* within the *"possibilities organization."*

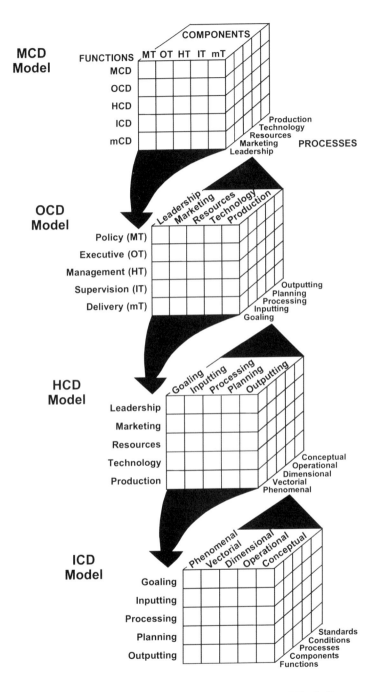

Figure 5-16. MCD–OCD–HCD–ICD Models

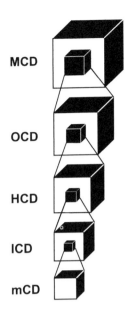

MCD

OCD

HCD

ICD

mCD

6 Managing Mechanical Capital Development

*Mechanical tooling is
the synergistic partner
of information
modeling.*

"Information-Driven mCD"
—Continuous Tooling

Mechanical automation began with wheels and belts driven by the forces of water and steam; later, electricity supplied the power. Now, mechanical automation is driven by the power of an intermediary force: information itself. Before computerization, people planned the operations of their machinery with paper mechanical drawings. They would designate a number of semi-automated processes for each of several machine stations. Then, at each station, people performed in tandem with the machinery to complete the processes. These people were, in fact, extensions of their machines. It was human intervention that was critical to the performance of nearly every mechanical step.

Manufacturing took a bold step in automation with the use of computers and CAD software for computer-assisted design (see Figure 6-1). With CAD software, mechanical drawings would be made in digital format, thus making mechanical design information easy to modify and distribute.

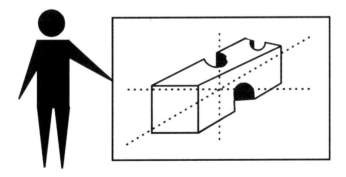

Figure 6-1. CAD—Computer-Assisted Design

Soon afterwards, manufacturing took another, still bolder step with CAM, or computer-assisted manufacturing—the marriage of digital design information with numerically controlled machinery (see Figure 6-2). Now information was directly driving machinery. Digital information, derived from CAD drawings, directed the operations of motors, valves, and electrical circuitry. With the availability of inexpensive software and computer hardware, digital information was now driving mechanical performance.

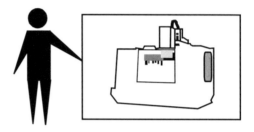

Figure 6-2. CAM—Computer-Assisted Manufacturing

Today, a few leading companies are expanding the power of their CAD-CAM design and manufacturing software with breakthroughs in information integration and automated engineering analyses. With information needed to undertake product development, activities can now be made available in an integrated form. Upstream from computer-assisted design and machining, the most powerful CAD-CAM systems can deliver all manner of integrated manufacturing information to managers and engineers, partners, suppliers, and even customers. An assembly-centric approach is used to relate product and process information in terms of information hierarchies. Then, with sophisticated information-navigation tools, these software systems deliver information such as process workflow; structural views, including 3D solid and stick drawings, piping, and electrical circuits; and parts and assemblies.

In addition, engineering modules of CAD software can also analyze potential design problems such as comparative weight calculations, interference detection related to the realities of assembly, and stress design analyses. With the click of a mouse, the software analyzes and then reports based upon digital design information. All of this before a single mold is poured, before a single part is manufactured!

What is the impact of this information-driven approach upon manufacturing? It can be considerable. For example, using this CAD-CAM software, Volvo cut its development time in designing and building a new bus from 4½ years to 18 months, and required only half the number of engineers it normally used. The linking and accessing of relevant manufacturing information and the application of tools for automated engineering analysis are breakthroughs in CAD-CAM information-driven mechanical capital development (mCD).

Without doubt, tremendous benefits accrue from the application of these CAD-CAM technologies. To date, the full power of these applications has not yet been installed extensively across the manufacturing marketplace. These CAD-CAM systems continue to serve as a source of competitive advantage for leading companies who have adopted these technologies.

Despite the availability of such innovations, managers who are responsible for the growth of their manufacturing companies must also look to the future and ask, "What breakthroughs in automation lie beyond CAD-CAM?" Even managers in service industries must ask similar questions: "How will the future of automation impact upon my business? How will it impact upon my customers?" Responses to these questions can be found in a study of mCD.

The future of automation is the development of information-driven mechanical tools to support operations that are upstream from CAD-CAM, namely: computer-assisted innovation, computer-assisted organization, and computer-assisted positioning in the marketplace (see Figure 6-3).

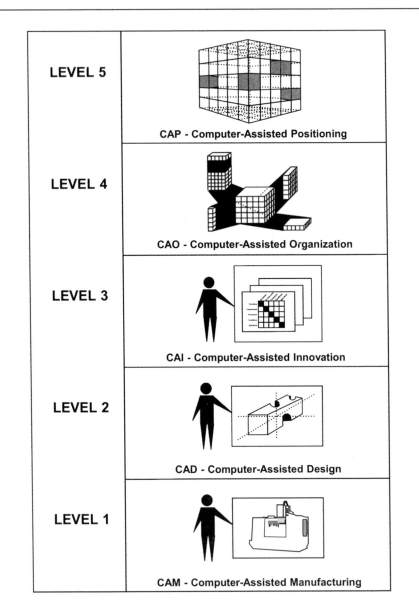

Figure 6-3. CAD-CAM Driven by Computer-Assisted Positioning, Organization, and Innovation Software

CAI—Computer-Assisted Innovation

Upstream from CAD, design engineers must bring innovative thinking to bear upon their product designs. Innovative thinking is the source of new product differentiation and new product benefits: in the context of global competitiveness, it is now a requirement of business. To build computer-assisted innovation (CAI) systems, the systems designers must understand innovation processes as well as which processes might be best served by automated tools (see Figure 6-4). In this regard, several such tools are being developed. For example, a simple yet powerful "systematic transfer" module provides automation support for a part of the innovation process. Linked to a database of product design information, the "systematic transfer" module populates tables of design information and supports automated variable manipulation strategies for prototyping design alternatives. Other CAI modules include decision support systems, simulation and scenario testing, and performance job aids.

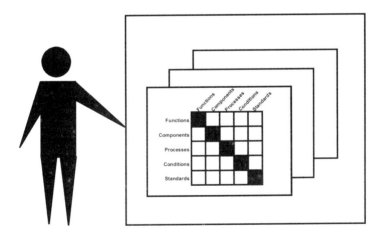

Figure 6-4. CAI—Computer-Assisted Innovation

CAO—Computer-Assisted Organization

Large or small, the organization is the context within which everyone works. Computer-assisted organization (CAO) tools service the distribution and alignment of goals, resources, processes, design plans, and production information within the context of the organization (see Figure 6-5). CAO software is designed to service the alignment of the entire enterprise. For example, CAO software will guide users to generate and operate within a "virtual organization." This virtual organization is a computer model that represents the assumptive world of the organization and its decision-makers. Once the model is customized, users may then interrogate the system with hypothetical organizational decisions regarding goals, resources, processes, plans, and production information. An automated analysis module generates implications and advice. The software also enables the routing of relevant information across an enterprise, based upon decisions made by users. Other CAO modules include Project Map, Asset Tracking, IC Router, and IC Team.

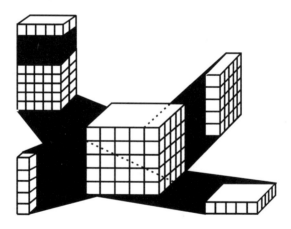

Figure 6-5. CAO—Computer-Assisted Organization

CAP—Computer-Assisted Positioning

"It's all in the positioning!" You may think that you are part of a well-aligned organization of terrific people, enabled by timely, accurate, and useful information, all in the service of providing the best products and services available in your specialty marketplace. Yet, without perspective regarding "positioning," you do not know how your organization, its people, its information, and its products and services measure up against the competition. Computer-assisted positioning (CAP) is a software tool for proactively addressing these positioning issues (see Figure 6-6). Reactively, it may also assist in repositioning products and services, as well as organizational resources. For example, users are assisted in generating a map of their specialty markets by defining current and projected customer requirements. Then, users measure the capabilities of their organizations against these market requirements. This information serves as a gateway into customized modules of positioning processes. Other CAP modules include Partnership Capital Positioning, Organizational Capital Positioning, Human Capital Positioning, Information Capital Positioning, and Machine Capital Positioning.

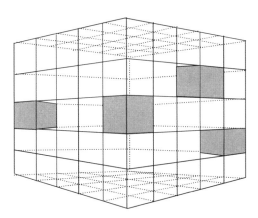

Figure 6-6. CAP—Computer-Assisted Positioning

We need look no further than the age in which we live to comprehend the awesome power of mechanical applications. Not only did mechanical tools culminate the Industrial Age in the Data Age, they also provided the data-processing platform upon which the Information Age is still being built. Entirely new industries and markets were generated by these machines. Among these machines, none were more powerful in their leveraged contributions than the integrated circuit, or semi-conductor chip.

Indeed, the chip may be viewed as a model for a great new age of productivity. This mechanical tool involves infinitesimal resource inputs and, in turn, yields potentially infinite results outputs. Essentially, the very age in which we live is a product of a tiny mechanical tool. The future ages which we generate will be enabled by the mechanical tools we are now developing. We can readily see how mechanical capital development (mCD) drives marketplace capital development (MCD) in opening up new markets. The greatest generator of wealth in the history of the world, mCD is the foundation upon which all of our other technologies are built.

Mechanical capital development must be seen in the perspective of all the other capital development systems in which it is nested. Mechanical capital development is the interaction of simple linear mechanical processes. Today, for example, the most sophisticated information tools and machines are driven by complex branching information-system designs. Information systems, in turn, are generated by human systems in order to serve organizational functions in relation to positioning in the marketplace. All products and services, at some level, are mechanically produced. Even this book! When we produce it mechanically, we are *doing it right*. The other conditions of new capital development tell us whether we are doing *the right thing*.

All *breakthroughs* in our understanding of mechanical processes lead directly to new phenomenal perspectives. The real *"capital"* value of mCD comes from the *"windows on phenomena"* that mechanical technologies deliver to us. Just consider all of the *"capital"* value that has been generated as a result of the mechanical breakthroughs of basic science. Our daily lives are powerfully impacted by practical product and service applications based upon mCD, the mechanics of our world.

The processes of mechanical capital development and information capital development are synergistic. As one grows, so does the other (see Figure 6-7). We may actualize mCD as a user of machinery or as a developer of it.

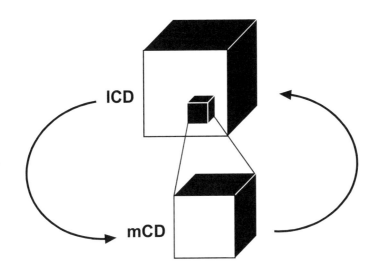

Figure 6-7. Synergistic Growth of Information and Machine Capital

Information designs are actualized with the development of machinery. We may then capitalize upon this mechanical capital as a source of wealth when we use or apply the most appropriate of the mechanical tools that are available to us. For most of us, this is how we can best use mechanical capital as a source of wealth generation. If we have a clear and useful understanding of what mCD is, and if we can accurately envision our needs and opportunities for the application of machinery, then, as machine users, we can apply mechanical capital as a source of comparative advantage. As machine users, we will find that the comparative advantage of machinery is of limited duration but must not be overlooked. The best use of available mechanical capital soon becomes new standards of operations for all of the organizations in our market segments.

Breakthroughs in machinery, or mechanical capital, may lead to new information designs, or information capital. In this situation, we may capitalize upon mechanical breakthroughs by generating new designs that will ultimately result in new machines. For those of us who define our organizations as machine developers, this is our way of leveraging mechanical capital as a source of comparative advantage. Here too, if we can clearly define our understanding of what mCD is, and if we can accurately envision the marketplace needs and opportunities for new machinery, then, as machine developers, we will be able to harness mechanical capital as a source of comparative advantage.

This chapter will introduce the critical dimensions of mechanical capital development by defining how we can model mCD and manage it as users or developers. The process of modeling and managing mCD is, itself, a source of wealth generation and comparative advantage.

MODELING MECHANICAL TOOLING

From early human interventions in the mechanics of planting, animal breeding, and metal forging to today's material sciences and bio-technologies, humanity has been harnessing mechanical processes. What were once considered naturalistic and probabilistic mechanical processes are now subject to the intentions and interventions of humanity. These interventions are all derived from the creative capabilities of the most possibilistic of all of nature's entities: the human being. These intentions of humanity are defined by information designs (ICD) to be actualized by mechanical performance (mCD).

From an operational perspective, it can be said that everything is, at its most elemental level, physical or mechanical. Processes for developing physical performance may be called mechanical capital development, or mCD. Probabilities processes describe, predict, and control mCD. Possibilities processes relate, empower, and free mCD. Whether our intentions are to control mCD or to free it, we begin to understand mCD by modeling its operations: its functions, components, and processes; its interdependent conditions, or contexts; and its standards of performance or sub-processes or sub-forces.

We build a model of mechanical capital by representing its functions, or intentions; its components, or parts; and its transformation processes, or how the mechanical components service the functions. The functions of mechanical capital development are defined by what it is intended to accomplish. Mechanical components are defined by their ingredients and how these ingredients are related. The processes of mechanical tooling are defined as the methods that apply mechanical capabilities in service of the tooling's intended purposes.

Equipped with the information above, we can construct a three-dimensional model for representing the functions, components, and processes of mechanical capital development. This model will serve us in our responsibilities to develop and manage mechanical tooling. We label our model "mCD," or "mechanical capital development." Building it involves four general steps:

1. Scaling the functions, or intentions, of machine performance;

2. Scaling the components, or parts, of mechanical capital that will service these functions;

3. Scaling the transformation processes that can be applied to mechanical components so they are able to complete their responsibilities;

4. Representing the interaction of these elements of mCD in a three-dimensional way.

A demonstration of how to carry out these steps will be provided in the following pages.

Once we understand how to model mCD, we will be able to manage our mechanical-tooling responsibilities by using our mCD model. We will begin to manage our mechanical tooling by scaling our information about mechanical capital development. We will cross information about machine components with information about mechanical functions to develop matrices of information about mechanical capital development. By bringing these into interaction with a third scale, the transformation processes of mechanical capital development, we will develop three-dimensional models of mechanical capital. Scaling, matrixing, and modeling provides useful methods for developing and managing the application of our mechanical capabilities.

Our model building will help us answer critical questions about mechanical capital development. Those questions include:

- *How do we generate and represent our mechanical abilities?*

- *What are our current methods and policies regarding the modeling of our mechanical capital resources?*

- *What current practices are effective?*

- *What are we missing?*

- *Are our machines available?*

- *Are our various mechanical capabilities related?*

- *Are our standards of performance in mechanical capital development aligned with the expectations and requirements of our customers?*

The growth and life of our mechanical capabilities, the information designs that drive our machinery, the human initiatives that develop our information designs, our organizations, and, ultimately, our positioning in the marketplace are all dependent upon our answers to these questions.

Scaling Information Functions

The functions, or intentions, of machinery are to fulfill information designs. Another way to say this is that the purpose of machinery is to serve information modeling. To describe these functions, we look to our information capital development (ICD) model. We derive the functions of machinery from the components of our ICD model, as shown in Table 6-1. We may note that the functions, or intentions, emphasize the levels of ICD modeling: phenomenal, vectorial, dimensional, operational, and conceptual. These information designs represent our mCD intentions.

Table 6-1. ICD Functions

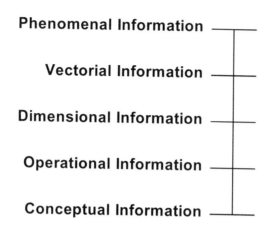

Phenomenal Information

Vectorial Information

Dimensional Information

Operational Information

Conceptual Information

This scale of machine functions is a useful initial *map-in* to orient us to the intentions of mechanical capital. Further analyses of each level of these functions will provide a deeper understanding and a more clearly defined description of the specific intentions we may have for machinery. As we learn more about each of these levels of requirements for information modeling, we will further define the functions, or intentions, of machinery.

By defining the functions of machinery, we begin to see the imbedded requirements. Does the machinery fulfill information models? If our machines do fulfill our information designs, then we may take a closer look at the quality of our component parts.

Scaling Mechanical Components

The next step in modeling mCD is to define its components, or ingredients. (Later sections in this chapter will explain what we mean by these mechanical components.) The components are shown in Table 6-2. As we may recall, they were previously introduced as the enabling processes in our ICD model. They provide a description of "basic science" (physics), and are needed to comprehensively describe the mechanical operations of phenomena. Once we have fully described these operations, we may then select to intervene in the mechanics of our world.

Table 6-2. mCD Components

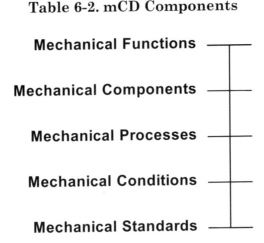

Mechanical Functions

Mechanical Components

Mechanical Processes

Mechanical Conditions

Mechanical Standards

The mCD components are described by their operations:

- **Mechanical functions,** or mechanical outputs, define the components of mechanical capital development.

- **Mechanical components** are the parts, or ingredients, dedicated to the mechanical functions.

- **Mechanical processes** are the mechanical procedures that transform the components into functions.

- **Mechanical conditions** are the mechanical environments within which the mechanical operations are performed.

- **Mechanical standards** of performance are the measures of sub-processes or sub-forces in operation.

These mCD dimensions are incorporated in multidimensional modeling: a three-dimensional phenomenal model is *nested* in a three-dimensional conditions model; in the three-dimensional phenomenal model are *nested* three-dimensional standards models.

Our scale of information about mechanical components is a useful initial *map-in* for analyzing the quality of our machinery. Further analyses of our mechanical capabilities in each area of mechanical operations will provide us with a more detailed description of the kinds of machinery we may want or need to develop.

Essentially, by defining the components of machinery, we have tools for analyzing the quality of our machines. Do they best serve their intended purposes? If not, then we should consider changing them.

Mechanical Capital Matrix

We begin to see the value of modeling our mechanical capital when we represent machine components, or ingredients, in relation to their functions, or intentions. We do this by creating what we call the Mechanical Capital Matrix (see Table 6-3). This matrix presents us with a visual model of how mechanical components are aligned to fulfill multiple levels of information intentions. In other words, it shows us that the mCD functions are discharged by the operational components of mCD.

Table 6-3. Mechanical Capital Matrix

COMPONENTS

FUNCTIONS	Functions	Components	Processes	Conditions	Standards
Phenomenal					
Vectorial					
Dimensional					
Operational					
Conceptual					

With the Mechanical Capital Matrix, we begin to see the distribution of our information and its intentions. This matrix should stimulate many important questions about the quality and availability of the machinery that we have or need in order to fulfill information designs. With this window on our machinery, we may begin to build our *mechanical capital*.

Scaling Mechanical Processes

The next step in building our mCD model is to introduce the transformation processes of mechanical capital development. As shown in Table 6-4, these processes include the following: programming (design), instructing (direction), tasking (objectives), steps (sub-objectives), and implementation (substeps).

Table 6-4. Mechanical mCD′ Processes

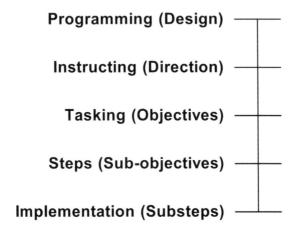

Programming (Design)

Instructing (Direction)

Tasking (Objectives)

Steps (Sub-objectives)

Implementation (Substeps)

The mCD′ processes are the means by which mCD components discharge mCD functions. We can see these processes at work in the next illustration (Figure 6-8). Basically, the mCD′ processes emphasize programmatic tasks and steps to achieve systems objectives.

The transformation processes provide the final piece of our model of ICD.

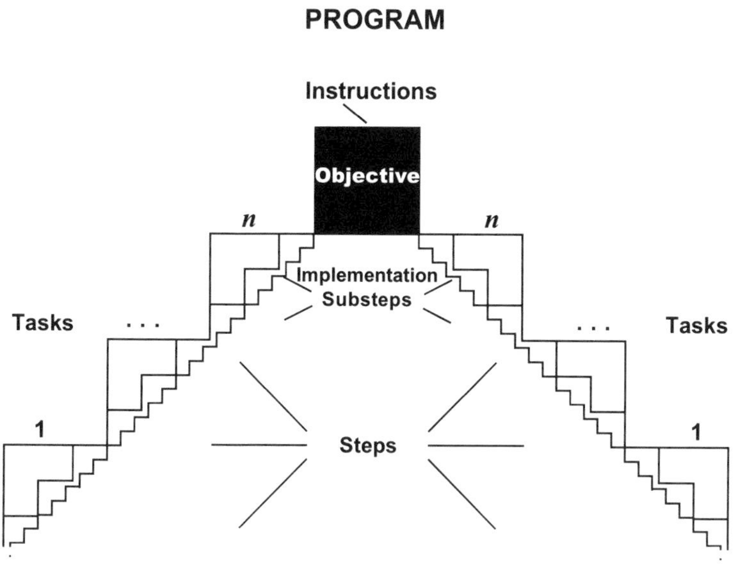

PROGRAM

Figure 6-8. Programmatic mCD′ Processes

mCD Model

We complete our mCD model by adding the processes of mechanical transformation (see Figure 6-9). The objective of the mCD model may be succinctly expressed as follows:

The functions, or intentions, of information modeling are fulfilled by mechanical components enabled by mechanical processes.

As may be noted, mechanical processes (mCD′) emphasize the linear processes that enable mechanical components (mCD) to discharge the intentions of information models (ICD). In other words, ICD functions are discharged by mCD components enabled by mCD′ processes.

We begin mechanical capital analysis and development by scaling, matrixing, and modeling our information about our machinery using the mCD model. Once we have modeled our current mechanical information, we will analyze its quality and

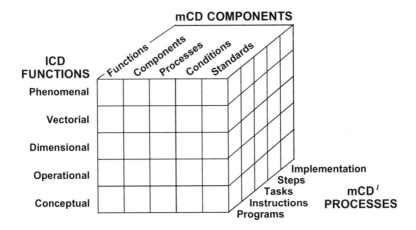

Figure 6-9. mCD Model

availability. Without a comprehensive understanding of mechanical capital, we are missing huge opportunities for developing and aligning the machinery needed to grow our organizations. With an understanding of mechanical capital, we may use this information to elevate our people and their information designs, and so maximize these contributions within the context of our aligned and marketplace-positioned organizations.

Next, we will focus upon better understanding mechanical components. In this way, we may improve our processes for performing with and managing our *mechanical capital,* and for developing it as the powerful source of wealth it can become.

PROCESSES FOR MECHANICAL TOOLING

Many businesses today are dedicated to delivering products that are the result of machine processes or the result of services with highly *"machine-like,"* repetitive processes. It is easy to see why the products of machine processes can be called mechanical capital development. But what about services performed by people? In this context, we must remember that such services may be mechanical as well—that people may, themselves, serve as machines. Thus highly repetitive services may also be called mechanical capital development.

206

How can we systematically intervene in the development and delivery of these mechanical products and services? How can we contribute to mechanical capital development? We can do so by *"mCD tooling."*

We initiate mCD tooling by mapping ourselves into the reasons for a mechanical intervention. The function (or goal) of every mechanical intervention is to actualize the intentions of someone as represented and communicated in an information design; this requires that we have a solid, working knowledge of systematic mechanical capital development.

Systematic mCD tooling is accomplished by intervening in the mechanical operations of phenomena. The mechanical operations of phenomena include all the ingredients that compose and define the phenomena. These ingredients include functions, components, processes, conditions, and standards. As shown in Figure 6-10, the component inputs are transformed into function outputs by processing. In turn, feedback represents performance standards. All of these operations exist with the boundaries of the system—a context of higher-order conditions. When we intervene in the mechanical operations of phenomena, we are intervening in one or more of these operational ingredients.

Conditions

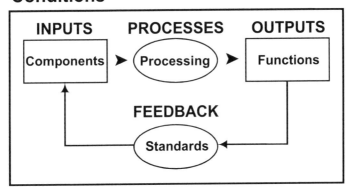

Figure 6-10. Systems Representation of mCD Tooling Operations

Our tooling interventions may take any or all of these forms:

* ***Function Tooling***
When we intervene in the functionality of phenomena, we **modify their purposes or intentions**. With willful phenomena, we may be able to replace a natural intention with a learned one. With phenomena that are not willful, we may not be able to intervene so directly; instead, we may have to change some other mechanical operations, such as components or processes, in order to change the functions. What is important to note here is that the intervener is capable of modifying the functions of phenomena directly or indirectly.

* ***Component Tooling***
We may intervene by **changing mechanical components**. Component replacement is perhaps the most frequently applied mechanical intervention. For example, Thomas Edison and his colleagues tried hundreds of different materials as filaments in their light bulbs before they found one that would be commercially viable. Change components, and we change phenomena!

* ***Process Tooling***
We may likewise **modify or replace the operational processes** of phenomena. Here we impact the mechanical system by focusing on transformational processes. For example, the entire pharmaceutical industry is built upon the idea of intervening in mechanical processes. Drugs are designed to block or enhance chemical and biological processes. Change processes, and we change phenomena!

* ***Conditions Tooling***
Mechanical conditions may also be changed. We may take the exact same phenomena and place them in new conditions and find that the phenomena now behave differently. For example: refrigeration slows food spoilage; certain crystals can grow in the weightlessness of outer space but not on earth; people suffer a high risk of pulmonary edema at elevations above 20 thousand feet. Change conditions, and we change phenomena!

- *Standards Tooling*
  Finally, we may also **modify the standards or sub-processes** of phenomena. This means impacting the operational physics of phenomena. For example, we may destabilize the phenomena's electromagnetic bonds and then restabilize them after infusing other component ingredients, thus creating a new product; this is what we do when we heat and cool tin and ore to create steel. Change standards of performance or sub-processes, and we change phenomena!

We can systematically consider our intervention options, and decide which to pursue, by using an *mCD transfer matrix* (see Figure 6-11). To process systematic mechanical interventions, we populate each dimension of the matrix with the operations of mechanical capital: functions, components, processes, conditions, standards. Then we systematically introduce options for consideration by holding some variables constant while modifying others.

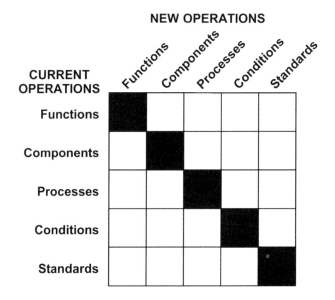

Figure 6-11. mCD Transfer Matrix

The choices we make result in the development of new forms of mechanical capital. With *breakthroughs* in mechanical operations, *breakthrough* information designs can be actualized. It is up to us to systematically apply these mCD tooling processes to develop mechanical capital.

IN TRANSITION

For a long period in history, the applications of mechanical capital development were found within the inflexible, monolithic assembly-lines and machines of mass production. Then, lacking the financial capital of Corporate America, Japan intervened in its assembly-line processes and issued the manufacturing challenge of the 1980s. Starting with inventories, the Japanese eliminated excesses until they arrived at "just-in-time manufacturing." By the 1990s, Corporate America had responded to Japan's challenge by incorporating "just-in-time manufacturing" and developing "agile manufacturing" systems.

Because agile manufacturing builds upon American assets in breakthrough thinking and technology development, it is now able to include new practices in the following areas of capital development:

 MCD practices to continuously position business constellations to become flexible and rapid strike forces in the marketplace.

 OCD practices to continuously align organizations to converge on problems and opportunities with teams that include customers, suppliers, and even competitors.

 HCD practices to continuously empower human capital to innovate and integrate solutions.

 ICD practices to continuously develop information in electronic formats, thus placing critical design expertise at hand with the click of a mouse.

Turning to information-driven mechanical tools, mCD machines to manufacture products and services. For example, using electronic link-ups, CAD-CAM systems can "drive" factory machines from electronic network sources miles away.

Mechanical capital makes its leveraged contribution when developed in relation to the higher-order capital systems in which it exists.

In short, by applying evolving capital development systems, *"possibilities corporations"* should be able to generate exponential improvements in manufacturing productivity and growth. The key to all this is interdependent processing between and within capital systems. Any one ingredient, such as mCD, is but an interdependent link in the food chain of capital development systems.

In all organizational delivery systems, mCD operates interdependently with all higher-order systems. The human capital systems engage in continuous interdependent processing to generate new possibilities images, which generate requirements for information capital modeling. These new and evolving information models generate requirements for new and evolving mechanical capital tools to implement these models. In turn, the human capital systems themselves are aligned to meet the requirements of organizational capital alignment and thus marketplace capital positioning.

This means that mCD is interdependently related to all capital development systems. Mechanical capital development systems are driven by the functions of higher-order capital development systems. These same mechanical capital systems, in turn, also drive the other capital development systems. For example, mechanical systems get an opportunity to drive marketplace systems. Those people responsible for mCD must process interdependently with the MCD people regarding their mechanical potential to deliver products and services to the marketplace. It is here, in this interdependent interaction, that mCD has the greatest impact upon the future of the organization. The basic mCD question that we must answer is:

Do we have the best mechanical methodologies to meet new design requirements?

If not, we must discover them immediately.

In this context, then, managing mCD depends in part upon the business we are in. Usually we do not think about mechanical practices unless we are in manufacturing businesses. However, even in service industries, we must be prepared to manage mCD in order to deliver the highest levels of services to our customers. In addition, even if we are not in manufacturing businesses today, we may very well be partnered in such businesses tomorrow.

It is therefore highly worthwhile to consider the model for managing mCD illustrated in Table 6-5. We may note that the model includes these capacity levels:

- *Best data* about the alternative mCD practices immediately available;

- *Best practices* for commercial mCD;

- *Best practitioners* for solutions of problems in best mCD practices;

- *Best ideas* for innovating new mCD;

- *Best processes* for generating new mCD.

Table 6-5. mCD Management

CAPACITIES LEVELS	mCD REQUIREMENTS				
	FUNCTIONS	COMPONENTS	PROCESSES	CONDITIONS	STANDARDS
5 - Best Processes					
4 - Best Ideas					
3 - Best Practitioners					
2 - Best Practices					
1 - Best Data					

Clearly, it is most desirable to have all of these levels available. Processing from higher-order HCD and ICD requirements ensures we will stay on the *cutting edge* with *state-of-the-art* mechanical capital development. Basically, we must discriminate the levels of innovations to which we have access in terms of mCD requirements and mechanical operations: functions, components, processes, conditions, and standards. We assess the following levels of mCD in achieving our objectives:

- *Best data* for alternative mechanical operations;

- Surveyed *best practices* of mechanical operations;

- Integrated *best practitioners* of mechanical operations;

- Innovated *best ideas* programs about mechanical operations;

- Generated *best processes* to develop mechanical operations.

We begin to get serious about mCD when we survey for *best practices*. We get commercial when we integrate *best practitioners* with *best practices*. We get innovative when we solicit *best ideas* from experts. We get generative when we participate with experts in *best processes* for generating *best ideas*. Clearly, we are best positioned when we have elevated programs involving *best processes*. Most companies have, at best, *best practices*.

In summary, mCD components are dedicated to fulfilling or actualizing ICD designs and are enabled by mCD′ processes. By continuous mechanical capital development, we will continue to generate requirements for other new capital development: MCD, OCD, HCD, ICD (see Figure 6-12 on the following page).

Mechanical capital development takes responsibility for the production of products and delivery of services. As such, it is the recipient of the deductive requirements of higher-order capital development systems. As we have learned, it is also the driver of MCD and other systems. In this context, the mCD system is the flagship of a probabilities management system. Indeed, historically, mCD was, itself, the probabilities management system. In a simple and straightforward manner, it planned the production, produced the product, and delivered the services. In the twenty-first century, however, the capital development systems that will

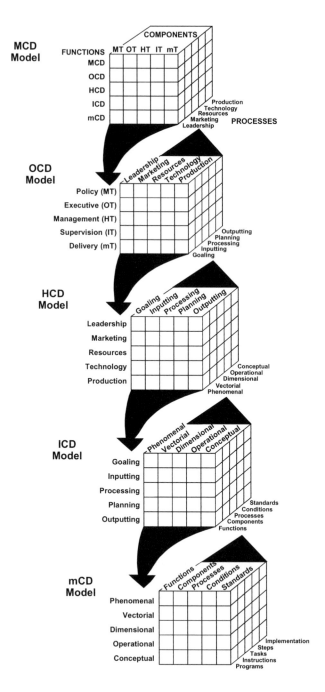

Figure 6-12. MCD–OCD–HCD–ICD–mCD Models

drive the organization will continually be in a state of change—as any of them may be the next driving source of economic growth.

In short, do not minimize the power of mCD and its probabilities processes. Do not *"throw the baby out with the bath water"!* Rather, maximize the power of mCD by developing a perspective on its importance and employment. The enduring function of probabilities systems is to complete the evolving vision of possibilities systems.

III

Summary and Transition

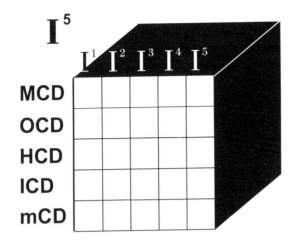

7 The Possibilities Management

The Possibilities
Management = NCD x I^5

"It's not about best technologies—it's about corporate culture change!" So reported the leaders of six of the largest multinational corporations. These reports are startling not so much for their insights as for the uniformity of their conclusions: *"Fifty percent of any deal-making is attributed to meeting culture-change require-ments and 50 percent to meeting best-technologies requirements!"*

The notion of culture-change requirements has been in the lexicon for a few decades now. Generally, these requirements are defined conceptually as "the need to overcome **resistance to change** due to a variety of hypothetical constructs." We may go further and operationally define the problem of culture change as:

The resistance to change due to the effects of conflicting reinforcement schedules generated by changing cultural conditions and measured by changing performance standards.

What this means is fairly simple: people do what they are rein-forced to do. They are *"captured"* by their reinforcement schedules and thus resistant to the introduction of new reinforcement sched-ules. They experience the new schedules as the downside of *"cul-ture shock"*: they feel punished for behavior that was previously rewarded; responses that were once meaningful are now neglected. Moreover, people regard the new schedules as beyond their control. Clearly, this view places culture-change resistance in the affective realm, seated in an emotional unwillingness to change.

Our own extensive, original research into the problem of change has yielded some simple yet profound conclusions. Behav-ioral change was, at one time, defined as requiring *"personality change."* In short, according to this notion, new behaviors could not even be considered until old behaviors had been thoroughly explored; consequently, endless months and years of treatment were needed to gain and incorporate insights into old patterns of behavior. With its emphasis on the past, the *"personality change"* hypothesis missed two related, vital integers of the present: the role of knowledge and the role of skills.

Our research, in recognizing these roles, has yielded a new method for personal change. We call this method *"training as treatment."* Our hypothesis holds that dysfunctional behavior, such as resistance to change, is caused by a deficit in either or both knowledge and skills; thus, new functional behaviors replace old dysfunctional ones when people are educated and empowered with knowledge and skills. Of course, some few individuals do not respond to training alone; for example, people with biochemical deficits require biochemical treatment. But for most people, the preferred mode of treatment is "training." Inhibition to change may be defined as *a problem of the affect,* but it can be overcome by *the power of the intellect* through knowledge and skills training.

We may well realize that culture change is a crucial issue facing every organization. In our hearts, we believe that change is possible. In our minds, we know that the training of our people is the preferred method for enabling change. But what is the most leveraged change curriculum for performance in the twenty-first century and beyond? What knowledge and skills will change our organizations and empower them to grow?

What follows are the Possibilities Management Systems (see Table 7-1), which present a road map for developing a "culture of change." It is a "possibilities curriculum." It will serve to orient our employees and our organizations to possibilities thinking in a possibilities organization. Along the left-hand column are the new capital development systems of *the possibilities organization.* These are the functions of every organization, to grow new capital development systems. Across the top of this matrix are the interdependent processing systems we call *possibilities leadership.*

What results can we expect if we empower our people with knowledge of, and skills in, new capital development and interdependent processing?

Let's begin with empowerment in new capital development, or NCD, systems. At some level, our employees are already considering NCD issues: marketplace, organization, human, information, mechanical. They do so, however, non-systematically and less than comprehensively. With a knowledge of NCD models and skills, performance will be elevated and culture change will be enabled. Overall, NCD models and skills will stimulate a change in the content and process of what happens at every level of the organization.

224

Table 7-1. The Possibilities Management Systems

POSSIBILITIES ORGANIZATION SYSTEMS	POSSIBILITIES LEADERSHIP SYSTEMS				
	I^1	I^2	I^3	I^4	I^5
MCD	Positioning by I^1	Positioning by I^2	Positioning by I^3	Positioning by I^4	Positioning by I^5
OCD	Aligning by I^1	Aligning by I^2	Aligning by I^3	Aligning by I^4	Aligning by I^5
HCD	Processing by I^1	Processing by I^2	Processing by I^3	Processing by I^4	Processing by I^5
ICD	Modeling by I^1	Modeling by I^2	Modeling by I^3	Modeling by I^4	Modeling by I^5
mCD	Tooling by I^1	Tooling by I^2	Tooling by I^3	Tooling by I^4	Tooling by I^5

Specifically, the requirements for marketplace positioning will finally have structure and form. By understanding the operations of the MCD model, we will raise new issues regarding the technological capabilities of the organization. Now marketplace requirements are defined in new ways; many questions arise about positioning in relation to the scale of generator through attenuator. At last, marketplace-positioning skills are defined: requirements, capabilities, mission, vision, model.

Organizational alignment is now explained with new depth. Discussions take form around the systematic flow of information across a system of organizational units and levels. New insights are made into the use of top-down deductive organizational processes as well as bottom-up inductive flows. Those responsible for "architecting" the structure of the organization have new ways of modeling and therefore managing the distributed processes of the organization.

We will also find that "human capital development" is no longer just another term for people; now it is defined by five sets of processing skills. The intellectual processing skills for which people have expressed a need are defined as observable, repeatable, teachable, and, most important, powerful skills—the skills of information relating, information representing, and processing individually, interpersonally, and interdependently.

Similarly, our requirements for information will be elevated. For example, conceptualizing will be acceptable in getting us started in our communications, but it will not be long before we find scales, matrices, 3D models, and vectorial and phenomenal information representations commonly in use in our organizations. With the development of new databases of information capital development, knowledge management will take on new meaning.

Finally, from our mechanical capital development model, we will learn new constructs to describe systematic processes for mechanical capital design and development.

Now let us anticipate the cultural-change results from empowerment in I^5 processing skills. Certainly, at some level, our employees are already processing, or thinking. As we know, if we have not provided our people with training in these skills, our current strategies are less than systematic and less than comprehensive. With knowledge of I^5 skills, systematic processes can be applied to problems and opportunities. Employees will learn skills for relating and representing information, and for processing their information environments individually, interpersonally, and interdependently. Facility in these processing skills will have an impact on performance at every level of the organization.

Possibilities management begins with I^1, information-relating skills. Ask your employees to describe their current approach, and you will find they have difficulty doing so. Information-relating skills enable us to transform conceptual information into operational information. Nothing is possible without skilled relating.

After I^2 skills training, our employees will represent information in a different way. They will now transform their information-relating experiences into new, better, factored, information products. They will apply skills to representing information: conceptually, operationally, dimensionally, vectorially, and phenomenally. These skills empower a revolutionary change in the quality of information that will be developed and made available.

We can expect to see creativity and generativity in our organizations. We will expect it because we will train for it. With I^3 skills for individual processing, new processes are introduced for goal-setting, analysis, and synthesis, as well as operationalizing and technologizing.

With I^4 skills, our employees will have a systematic approach for interpersonal processing with others. These are the interpersonal processing skills of goaling, getting, giving, growing, and going. Their interaction with individual processing skills leads to the skilled co-processing or collaboration that is now a requirement of our employees.

Finally, with I^5 skills our employees will learn how to *"live in the houses that they build."* In short, they will learn how to process interdependently with any information or any phenomena. They will generate to build these houses and innovate inside these houses.

The matrix for new capital development and I^5 skills means that our employees will apply I^5 skills in service of new capital development requirements. This is the curriculum for developing a possibilities culture and enabling the change or growth that defines a possibilities organization.

Managing NCD

We conclude this work by illustrating how we become *"one"* with the customer's organizational cells; in other words, how we process interdependently within these units. Let us focus on an organization that includes all of the levels of new capital development: MCD, OCD, HCD, ICD, mCD (see Figure 7-1).

The organizational **functions** that account for these NCD systems are driven by marketplace processing. We may note that those functions are policymaking, executive architecture, management systems, supervisory objectives, and delivery tasks.

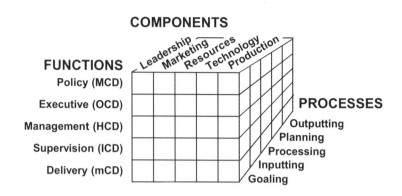

Figure 7-1. Organizational Model

The organizational **components** that discharge these functions are driven by organizational processing: they include leadership, marketing, resources (and their integration), technology, and production. Finally, the empowering **processes** that enable the components to discharge the functions are driven by human processing: they include goaling, inputting, processing, planning, and outputting.

Now let us map ourselves into a cell in the organization. We are going to choose the marketing component dedicated to the policymaking, MCD function (see Figure 7-2). We are also going to include all of the phases of organizational processing accomplished by humans. How are we going to process interdependently within this cell?

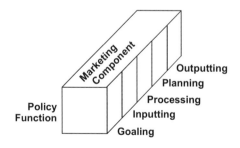

Figure 7-2. Marketing Component

First of all, as members of the marketing component, we have already processed interdependently with leadership and all other components to generate our positioning in the marketplace:

To accomplish ICD and mCD requirements by IT and mT corporate capacities in commoditization and attenuation markets.

As part of our goaling process in marketing, we will engage in continuous interdependent processing of this marketplace positioning with all other components. Our corporate positioning is illustrated in Figure 7-3.

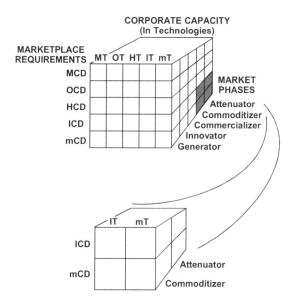

**Figure 7-3. Corporate Positioning
in the Marketplace (Goaling Phase)**

As part of our inputting process in marketing, we will engage in continuous interdependent processing with our customer organizations. We will discover what their positioning is: their requirements, their capacities, their markets.

In many instances, their positioning in the marketplace will be similar to ours. However, with interdependent processing, we may discover that they are increasingly aware of the need to develop the internal capacities of other technologies (HT, OT, MT) in order to achieve their ICD and mCD requirements (see Figure 7-4).

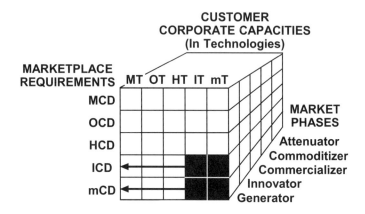

**Figure 7-4. Customer Needs Assessment
(Inputting Phase)**

In the processing phase of marketing, we may process interdependently to generate entirely new images of our relationship with our customers. We may recognize that their needs are our needs. We may dedicate developmental efforts to producing technological capacities that empower our customers to meet their marketplace requirements (see Figure 7-5). Knowing we are related interdependently to our customers' growth, we may modify our original positioning to become *"Relationship Marketing"*: basically, we empower our customers in the capacities they require to succeed; moreover, we empower our customers in the capacities they require to continue to be our customers. That way we grow together!

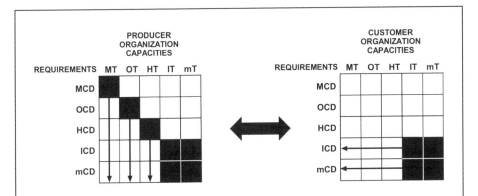

Figure 7-5. Relationship Marketing
(Processing Phase)

In the planning phase of marketing, then, we process interdependently to develop the empowerment design to develop
customer technological capacity to achieve marketplace
requirements (see Figure 7-6). As may be noted, the NCD
technology mission incorporates MT, OT, and HT goals and
their objectives.

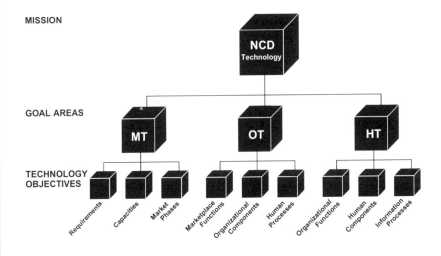

Figure 7-6. Empowerment Design
(Planning Phase)

Finally, the outputting phase of marketing emphasizes the outputs from the implementation of the empowerment design (see Figure 7-7). In this instance, the models for MT, OT, and HT capacities are the technological models we have reviewed in this work.

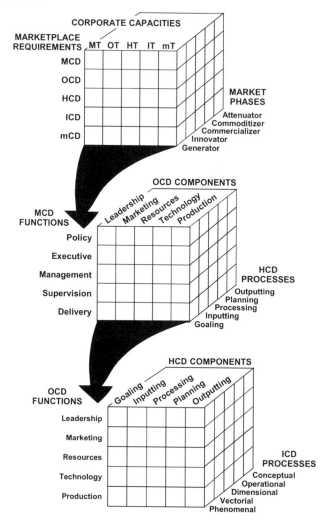

**Figure 7-7. NCD Technology Models
(Outputting Phase)**

In summary, by processing interdependently in our marketing component, we have accomplished the following:

- Corporate positioning by goaling;
- Customer needs assessment by inputting;
- Relationship marketing by processing;
- Empowerment design by planning;
- Technological capacity by outputting.

We have empowered the customer to meet its requirements in the marketplace. In so doing, we have elevated our own capacity for offering customers interdependent growth relationships.

All of this is not possible without interdependent processing, which is itself a set of human processing skills involving the following technological capacities:

- The information-relating capacities to generate operational images of phenomena;

- The information-representing capacities to generate dimensional images of phenomena;

- The individual-processing capacities to generate new images of phenomena;

- The interpersonal-processing capacities to generate more powerful images of phenomena;

- The interdependent-processing capacities to generate the most powerful images of phenomena.

These interdependent-process capacities are the keys to unlocking our mutual organizational growth potential. They define *"possibilities leadership."*

In Transition

Our economy and our organizations are driven by, and drivers of, *technological breakthroughs.* Our businesses may take advantage of the technological breakthroughs of others, or they may generate technological breakthroughs themselves. The success of our organizations is dependent upon how well we relate to "change": changing requirements, changing opportunities.

When our organization is holding to old ways, it is defining itself as following a *"probabilities paradigm."* It looks at past performance and hopes that current processes, products, and services, based upon old technologies, will continue to satisfy market requirements.

When our organization is *"pushing the envelope,"* asking itself and others for new processes, products, and services, it is defining itself as living the *"possibilities paradigm."* It looks at projections of future requirements and believes that new processes, products, and services, based upon technologies just discovered and soon to be discovered, will revolutionize how current requirements are satisfied. More important, possibilities processes introduce new requirements, ones that were never before thought possible or perhaps never even before conceived of!

We can embrace change. We can even become generators of change. When we adopt new capital development models and systems, we are opening ourselves to new possibilities. When we adopt systematic I⁵ Possibilities Management Systems, we are empowering the people in our organizations with skills for generating change.

So, we must ask ourselves who we want to become. Do we want to identify ourselves and our organizations as *"probabilities people"* in a *"probabilities organization"*? Or, do we dare ask ourselves and our organizations to become *"possibilities leaders"* generating a *"possibilities organization"*? In this book, we have delivered our vision of the **Possibilities Organization** and **Possibilities Leadership** technologies to enable the **Possibilities Organization.**

The choices are yours.

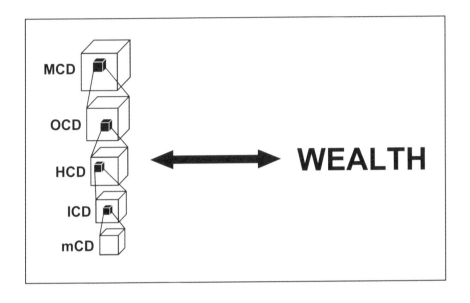

MCD

OCD

HCD

ICD

mCD

WEALTH

NCD ⟷ **WEALTH**

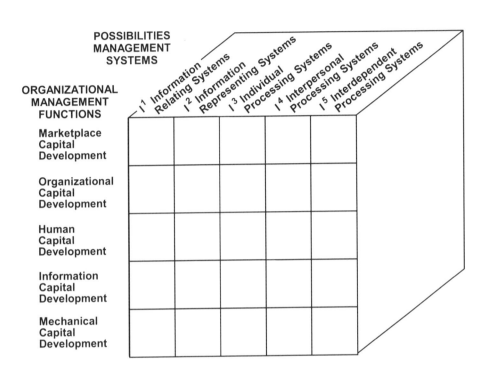

POSSIBILITIES
MANAGEMENT
SYSTEMS

ORGANIZATIONAL
MANAGEMENT
FUNCTIONS

Marketplace
Capital
Development

Organizational
Capital
Development

Human
Capital
Development

Information
Capital
Development

Mechanical
Capital
Development

I¹ Information
Relating Systems

I² Information
Representing Systems

I³ Individual
Processing Systems

I⁴ Interpersonal
Processing Systems

I⁵ Interdependent
Processing Systems

THE POSSIBILITIES
MANAGEMENT PARADIGM

Selected Publications by Authors

The Possibilities Leader. Amherst, MA: HRD Press, 2000.

The New Science of Possibilities. Volumes I & II. Amherst, MA: HRD Press, 2000.

The Possibilities Mind. Amherst, MA: HRD Press, 2000.

Human Possibilities. Amherst, MA: HRD Press, 2000.

Empowering. Amherst, MA: HRD Press, 1990.

The Age of the New Capitalism. Amherst, MA: HRD Press, 1988.

Human Processing and Human Productivity. Amherst, MA: HRD Press, 1986.

The Exemplar. Amherst, MA: HRD Press, 1984.

The Sources of Human Productivity. Amherst, MA: HRD Press, 1983.

Interpersonal Skills and Human Productivity. Amherst, MA: HRD Press, 1982.

Toward Actualizing Human Potential. Amherst, MA: HRD Press, 1981.

The Development of Human Resources. New York, NY: Holt, Rinehart & Winston, 1971.

Helping and Human Relations. Volumes I & II. New York, NY: Holt, Rinehart & Winston, 1969.

Acknowledgments

First, we would like to acknowledge the contributions of the core of research associates in Carkhuff Thinking Systems, Inc., who helped to develop some of the ideas presented in this work:

- Don Benoit, M.A., who contributed operations to information representation,
- Chris Carkhuff, M.A. Cert., who developed the organizational capital models,
- Alvin Cook, Ph.D., who built math models and coding systems,
- Barbara Emmert, Ph.D., who provided information systems perspective,
- Dave Meyers, M.A., who engineered organizational applications,
- Darren Tisdale, M.A., who innovated technological applications.

In addition, we owe a special debt to a number of people—themselves *"possibilities managers"* who made applications of our work at Human Technology, Inc.:

- John Cannon, Ph.D., Vice President, New Capital Development,
- Alex Douds, M.A., Director, Performance Systems Group,
- Sharon Fisher, M.A., Chief Operating Officer,
- Ted W. Friel, Ph.D., Information Technology Consultant,
- Richard Pierce, Ph.D., Director, Organizational Consulting Group.

We are particularly indebted to those scientists who contributed early on to our overall thinking:

- David N. Aspy, D.Ed., Carkhuff Institute,
- George Banks, D.Ed., Carkhuff Institute,
- David H. Berenson, Ph.D., Carkhuff Institute,
- Ralph Bierman, Ph.D., Carkhuff Institute,
- B. R. Bugelski, Ph.D., S.U.N.Y. at Buffalo,
- James Drasgow, Ph.D., S.U.N.Y. at Buffalo,
- Gerald Oliver, M.S., Carkhuff Institute,

- Flora N. Roebuck, D.Ed., Carkhuff Institute,
- Richard Sprinthall, Ph.D., American International College.

We also owe gratitude to pathfinders in business and industry who gave us opportunities to make applications:

- Rick Bellingham, Ph.D., Genzyme, Inc.,
- Russ Campanella, Genzyme, Inc.,
- Dave Champaign, Lotus Corp., IBM,
- Barry Cohen, Ph.D., Parametric Technology Corp.,
- John T. Kelly, M.A., IBM,
- Bill O'Brien, M.A., Parametric Technology Corp.,
- Russ Planitzer, Lazard, Inc.,
- Jack Riley, IBM,
- Peter Rayson, M.Sc., C. Eng., Parametric Technology Corp.,
- Carl Turner, General Electric,
- Norman Turner, General Electric.

We are also indebted to educational advisors with whom we processed interdependently to make extensive applications:

- Cheryl Aspy, D.Ed., University of Oklahoma,
- William Anthony, Ph.D., Boston University,
- Karen Banks, D.Ed., James Madison University,
- Sally Berenson, D.Ed., North Carolina State University,
- Terry Bergeson, Ph.D., Superintendent of Public Instruction, Washington,
- Mikal Cohen, Ph.D., Boston University,
- Andrew H. Griffin, D.Ed., Assistant Superintendent of Public Instruction, Washington,
- Shirley McCune, Ph.D., Assistant Superintendent of Public Instruction, Washington,
- Jeannette Tamagini, Ph.D., Rhode Island College.

Also, we express our gratitude to the trainers of Human Capital Development at the HRD Center, American International College, for piloting some of our work:

- Debbie Decker Anderson, D.Ed., Director,
- Cindy Littlefield, M.A., Associate Director,
- Susan Mackler, M.A., Holyoke Community College,
- Richard Muise, M.A., Assistant Director.

There are those who deserve our appreciation for their support in transforming these early manuscripts into readable books:

- Dave Burleigh, D B Associates for Marketing,
- Bob Carkhuff, HRD Press, for positioning,
- John Cannon, Ph.D., Human Technology, Inc., for his critical readings,
- Mary George, M.A., HRD Press, for editing.

Jean Miller deserves an exceptional note of recognition for implementing our *"rapid prototyping"* method of writing: about one dozen versions of each book were produced before final copy. Not only did she turn around high-quality typing, she also turned around high quality with timeliness. Not only did she generate creative graphics and layout, she also continuously retrieved lost files and, on at least two occasions, tracked down misdelivered manuscripts. These books are as much her books as ours!

Finally, we owe a debt of everlasting love and gratitude to those people who have been absolute in their commitment to enabling us to actualize our vision: our wives, Bernice and Gloria, who related to our experience, empowered our potential, and released us to the freedom of our scientific pursuits. For nearly 50 years, we have been saying, *"Give us another year and we'll get there."* Well, the *year* is up! And we got there!